MURDERS THAT SHOCKED BARBADOS

BY

Kim L Ramsay

Ramsay, Kim L.

Murders That Shocked Barbados

ISBN 978-976-8265-84-5

Printed and bound by COT Holdings Limited
Barbados, West Indies

Murders That Shocked Barbados by Kim L Ramsay

Contents

A WORD FROM THE AUTHOR ABOUT THE BOOK

Dear Readers,

L et me begin with my own confession. Writing this book was one of the most difficult decisions I have ever made. I have wrestled with the decision on and off for almost a year on whether or not to write this book because of the nature of it. Writing **Barbados' Most Wanted**, my first book, was much easier. That book was about 11 of Barbados' most notorious criminals who at some point terrorised Barbados and had the country in a state of fear while on the run, most of whom have gone to the great beyond in shoot outs with the police. While there should be no celebration about the demise of anyone, writing about them was easier.

Not this book. This book is about some of the island's most gruesome and horrific murders, some of which have never been solved. These cases involved suffering, grief, undetermined motives in some cases, heartache and loss of loved ones who were going about their business in their day to day activities, heading to or from work, church or play, relaxing at home, enjoying precious moments with loved ones, when they were brutally taken from their loved ones. These people did not deserve to die the way they did. They did not harm anyone. They were not notorious. They were not wanted. They were just innocent Barbadian citizens who, like me and you, had a legitimacy in being productive everyday people. They never had that chance to live their dreams.

One of my biggest challenge was getting through to the families of these victims, many of whom did not want to discuss their loved one, understandably so. Each person who was taken so tragically, left loved ones: a mother, father, brothers, sisters, partners, best friends who equally suffered a loss; they too are victims. Worse, in some of these stories, the deceased was not alone at the time of their death. These co-victims were also hurt physically and survived. They are just as much a victim as the deceased, and my heart goes out to them. I can only imagine what life could have been surviving and having a continued existence after such a tragedy.

It is not my intention to rehash pain and terrible memories of the death of their loved ones. On the contrary, this book is a memory of all victims, whether mentioned in this book or not, who have passed due to violence. In many cases, perpetrators do not consider the pain that they have caused, not only to their victims, but to their own families and partners who are also negatively affected by their nefarious actions.

To the families and loved ones of the 32 victims in this book, I, along with Barbados and the wider community feel your pain. Loss of any kind is not easy. It can take months, years and in some cases a lifetime of pain, suffering and despair for the pain to subside. It is even harder when there has been no closure.

This book is dedicated to these victims and their loved ones. It tells their story and hopefully some lessons which can be learnt to help someone who is facing or has faced such tragedy in their lives. May their souls rest in peace.

Kim Ramsay

FOREWORD

I deem it both a pleasure and a privilege to be asked to write the Foreword to such a wonderful book. In light of what has been occurring worldwide, and particularly in the United States, it is a very timely work. So when Kim mentioned to me that she was writing this book, I unhesitatingly agreed to write the foreword.

The Black Dahlia! The Brides in the Bath Case! The Zodiac Killer!

These are names or rather monikers of brutal murders which occurred in the US and the UK. Approximately, for the past 15 to 20 years, we in Barbados could be forgiven for believing that such things did not exist in our island.

But this seminal work of Kim Ramsay tells us otherwise. In fact, whether spoken of *sotto voce* or in whispered tones, this noted criminologist makes it clear that Barbados has had its fair share of shocking, gripping, riveting murders and, indeed, some unsolved ones as well. I will focus on only a few in this foreword, but I highly recommend the entire book.

One needs to be of a certain age to recall going off to church for the traditional 5:00 a.m. Christmas morning which always began with the lusty singing of the hymn "Christians Awake, Salute the Happy Morn" and recalling that on Christmas Day 1967, on returning home to hear the horrible report on Rediffusion that, while the Rector of St. Matthews, Rev. Charles Gale, was busily recounting the Christmas homily, with "glad tidings of great joy," his seven-months pregnant wife and their infant son were being brutally murdered.

And Kim tells it in a way that it is never too far from the mind on any early Christmas morning.

And if the US has its Black Dahlia, we have our own unsolved murder in the *'Pele'* Case. Kim tells the story in a way which shows the disparate directions in which the evidence takes us, all with suspicion but no solution. It, of course, does not help that the one person who probably knows more about it than any other living person now lives overseas.

More recently, the Campus Trendz killings of six innocent women by Molotov cocktails gripped the island as well as those in the diaspora. In fact, I was in New York at the time it happened.

For me, the value of this book is two-fold. In the case of each murder, Kim dissects the facts like a lawyer and puts them into perspective. Yet she avoids making the rendition dry and unexciting as we lawyers can do to even a lively story. It is this historical narrative, this weaving together of facts which, at first, appear unrelated, which make this book hard to put down once you have started reading it. And she leaves us with many conundrums. So, while in Brazil, the name *'Pele'* will always evoke *mastery*, the name *'Pele'* in Barbados will always evoke *mystery* and murder and, perhaps more painfully for the family of Victor Parris, the failure of our criminal justice system to solve a murder that cries out to be solved.

I suspect that many an hour will find me re-reading chapters and deriving an entirely different take on the facts. If nothing else, the enduring quality of this book for which I congratulate Kim will be this – that even after you have been able to put it down, you will go back to it.

One final observation. In the book, Kim has spent much time on the plight of the victims, including both survivors and family members. In her concluding remarks, she speaks to the need for the victims' rights and their voices to be considered, even if the ultimate result is not changed. I could not agree more. In my judgment, victims, no less than judges, jurors, prosecutors and defence counsel are part of the process, and must be treated as such. In the Practice Direction on Maximum Sentence Indications which are a form of guilty plea practice where the judge gives an indication of the likely sentence which the guilty pleader is likely to attract, provision is made for Victim Impact Statements to be considered. And in my view, it is important for virtual complainants, victims and their families to be notified by the court of such crucial events as sentencing and decisions on appeal. We have not done a great job of this – I must say *mea culpa*. But we will do better. That Kim has brought this issue to the fore as well makes the book a *must read*.

I unreservedly recommend this book.

Marston C. D. Gibson, K.A.
Chief Justice of Barbados.

ACKNOWLEDGEMENTS

This book could not have been possible without the help of the following persons:

First, I want to thank the Almighty Father for giving me the foresight, strength and perseverance to continue to write when I wanted to give up so many times.

I also want to thank Chief Justice Sir Marston Gibson for his Foreword, contributions, sharing of decisions and judgements and feedback on this book.

I could not have completed this book without the help of my editors, Paula Richards and Hopeton Peterson.

Thanks to Kathie Daniel of Southpaw Grafix for the design of the cover.

Thanks to Mel Yearwood for the layout of the book.

Thanks to the staff of the **Nation** newspaper and Barbados Advocate, particularly Monie Barrow, Antoinette Connell, Maria Bradshaw and Yvonne Norville.

Staff of the Criminal Justice Research and Planning Unit.

Credit to Charles Grant for some of the pictures in this book.

The Commissioner of Police and his Deputy Commissioner of Police, Erwin Boyce.

Ag Senior Superintendent Graham Husbands and Inspector Vernon Farrell of the Royal Barbados Police Force for your support and assistance.

Superintendent of Prisons, Colonel John Nurse and his staff for permission to interview some of the men mentioned in the book.

The late Keith Whittaker who up to the time of his untimely demise offered some information about some of the cases.

Sylvester 'Slater' Williams, retired Assistant Commissioner of Police, Royal Barbados Police Force.

Marilyn Rice Bowen of Barbados Association of Retired Persons (BARP).

Andrew Power for his guidance, support and poem.

Lady Mullion Q.C. for her legal opinion on the book.

My friends Alison Morgan, David Straughn, Patrick Gill, Correy Mitchell, Modupe Sodeyi-Boadu and Lusanne Payne-Gittens who have assisted, offered advice or have been a pillar of support throughout this journey.

And last but definitely not least, my darling family. Thank you always for being my tower of strength and for your unwavering support.

DISCLAIMER

The information contained in this book is drawn from a collection of newspaper reports, police records, interviews with retired police officers, prisoners and some family members of the victims.

Information provided through interviews and accounts cannot be verified in all cases.

ABOUT THE AUTHOR

K im Ramsay is a criminologist for the past 20 years having been trained at the University of Leicester in the United Kingdom.

She is a Senior Researcher with the Government of Barbados and has conducted research on issues related to crime and the criminal justice system. Her main research interests are penal policy, criminal justice reform and research on violence and violence prevention.

She has conducted research on homicides; gangs; recidivism of ex-prisoners; a public opinion survey on crime; juvenile delinquency and fear of crime.

Kim L. Ramsay

Kim is also a part time lecturer in Criminology at The University of the West Indies where she has been teaching on and off for approximately 20 years. She is also the author of the book *Barbados' Most Wanted; The Barbados Prison System: Chronicles of Death, Riots and Reformation; Sex, Drugs and Murder: Unsolved Murders in Barbados* and *The Unspoken: A Glimpse of the Dark Side Of Gang And Street Culture.*

INTRODUCTION

The loss of a loved one is never easy. It is even harder when that person is taken from their families through violent circumstances. The impact of murders affects families, friends, communities and the entire society, often for months and even years after the event. In a society where there are cries for justice for those left behind, many persons are left feeling victimised all over again when the wheels of justice move too slow, or in some cases seem to move only in favour of the perpetrator. Long delays, in some cases years, bail for the alleged perpetrator who can remain in society for years due to the slow movement of cases through the criminal justice system, appeals that can and do go on for years at the expense of tax payers, and landmark decisions which go in favour of accused persons.

Meanwhile, in what seems to be a paradox of life, the victims tend to be forgotten. They wait for years for justice, some of them suffer financial, social, and even psychological setbacks. The psychological scars, which are not visible to the average person or to the naked eye, sometimes never goes away.

Homicide Trends

Between 1980 and 2019, Barbados recorded approximately 874 murders. In 2019 alone, up to mid-August, Barbados recorded an unprecedented 34 homicides. While murder rates tended to be steady in the past 15 years, there has been a significant increase for the year so far.

In the 1980s and 1990s, Barbados witnessed several predatory murders, such as the canefield murders, where bodies of women were disposed of in places such as wells and cane fields, as well as other gruesome murders which were personal and more vicious in their execution. In more modern times, murders are usually driven by disputes between individuals, warring groups or factions and gangs, the drug trade and to some extent domestic violence. The easy accessibility to guns nowadays also changed the landscape of most of the murders.

Up to the mid to late 1980s, less than 20 persons were murdered in any given year. The nature of murders was different in the 1980s. In the early 1980s/1990s, there were predatory crimes which included rapes and assaults, resulting in horrific brutal murders especially of young women.

According to a homicide study by the National Task Force on Crime Prevention (Ramsay, 2011) from late 1980s (around 1987), the number of homicides started to increase and the circumstances and weapons surrounding these murders had started to shift over the years. The use of guns in the commission of murders has been on the increase since the late 1980s and has continued unabated since then.

In the early 1980s, knives and other sharp-edged tools were mostly used in murders. There was a significant decrease in sharp-edged tools from the mid to late 1980s and it continued to decrease, only recently rising once again in 2019.

This is a historical narrative of the murders of 32 persons who were killed in horrible circumstances over a time period of close to 80 years in Barbados. Of these persons who were killed, a significant portion of them were women (22 women, representing 71% of all the murders). Three men were killed and seven children ranging from unborn to 16 years old. There were countless victims of these crimes in the name of survivors who either witnessed or were attacked, but survived the particular incident that resulted in a murder. Some of these survivors were children themselves, as was the case of the Happy Cot murders.

The wider society moves on from the senseless killings and the public moves on to the next hot topic of the day which quickly envelops the headline story of the murder; after all, this is how societies operate. The world is a fast-moving solar system where the horrific murder of last week is taken over in the headlines by the new topic of tomorrow. However, for many families, the case never goes away. It is even worse when the murder is unsolved. In this book, there are eight unsolved murders, and one murder where a man was charged, but eventually acquitted. In these circumstances, it seems as though the families never got the closure of the death of their loved one.

While ALL murders are shocking and senseless, I have decided to focus on some cases which brought Barbadians to their knees in shock, fear and trepidation while demanding justice for the victims. Some of these cases have gone down in our history books as some of the most shocking and disturbing cases of murder the island has ever experienced. These murders caused a collective gasp of horror and awe at the mere brutality and senselessness of the crimes.

The book begins with looking at two cases, 50 years apart where two men went berserk in their communities and killed eight people between the two of them.

It then goes on to highlight murders spanning 43 years and these include the cane field murders, the Balls Plantation murder of Arlene Watts, the murder of Esther Skeete on her way to church, the murders of brother and sister Antonio and Kimberly Gilkes; the murders of Gillian Bayne and Amanda Newton who were dumped in wells, the murder of a 16 year old Russian girl named Anna; the Campus Trendz robbery and murders of six women and the famous 'Pele' Parris murder, which was steeped in political conspiracies, cover ups and love affairs, and which led to at least two calypso songs written about it.

While these 32 persons are no longer here with us, they have left countless friends, families, acquaintances and a wider society that still grapples with their deaths. It is not easy, even though time makes the pain subside, but it never goes away.

Here are the stories.

CRIME SCENE DO NOT CROSS

CHAPTER ONE

Deadly Insanity

T he stories are 50 years apart. The settings are both in small communities. Two men, both considered easy-going and quiet, went berserk one morning and murdered eight people between the two of them.

Haggatts, St Andrew (1933)

The idyllic, rural parish of St Andrew is well known for its utterly beautiful and magnificent scenery - rugged hilly coastlines, chalky hills and serenity. The Ermie Bourne Highway, provides a glimpse of this unique landscape, offering breathtaking views of the coastline dotted with the most picturesque beaches. It is a parish where many hikers are drawn because of its hilly landscape. But one February Thursday in 1933, the beauty of this scenic parish was marred by the brutal murders of five innocent people at the hands of a mad man.

Haggatts, a small district in the parish, is a popular starting point for hikers. Haggatts was a typical plantation village where most persons were labourers on the sugar plantation. The hub of plantation life was Haggatts Yard.

Long before its attraction as a hiking spot, Haggatts was notoriously known as the place where the gruesome murders occurred thanks to Seon Hope. Born in 1897, Hope, also known as Sow Hopey, was a Barbadian labourer who lived in the community in the 1930s with his family. On February 23 1933, referred to as "Bloody Thursday," Hope, armed with a machete, ran amok creating havoc and changed the course of history in the small rural district of Haggatts St Andrew. According to newspapers at the time, on February 22, 1933, Seon, who the Barbados Weekly referred to as "an ignorant labourer unable to read or write," quarrelled with his wife Coolie, because she had cooked food without giving him any – according to other sources, it was over the loss of a pound of flour.

One hour of terror

The argument abated only to continue at 9:30 a.m. the following morning. When he threatened to kill his wife with a pitchfork, she left their home to file a complaint at the District "F" Police Station. On her way there, she apparently changed her mind, returned, and called on island constable Fitz Collymore who she passed on the road.

During that time, Seon approached his wife and Constable Collymore from Haggatts' plantation yard and spoke with them for a while, before he drew a knife from his pocket and threatened to kill them. When Coolie then asked Collymore to witness for himself the threat against her life, Seon turned to leave, but he suddenly turned towards them again, and attacked his wife with the knife, injuring her in the head, hands, and body. When Collymore tried to intervene, Seon grabbed a baton from him and hit him on the head, while Coolie used the distraction of her husband to flee into a cane field, where she was later found unconscious. Seon eventually went home, threatening "I am going home for my machete; and when I come back all of you can look out!"

Haggatts Plantation Yard (now a depot)

Back home, Hope armed himself with the machete and travelled about a quarter of a mile towards Haggatts' yard, where he encountered Aileen Clarke washing clothes on a pasture not far from the road. Without saying a word, Seon fatally chopped her in the head and shoulders. Fifty yards further down the street, Hope saw island constable James Thompson and wounded him in the head and shoulders. At that time, labourers coming from work arrived at the scene, and when a manager named Mr Davis rode along the street, Hope told him not to be afraid. He then chased the labourers, who fled before him, but was unable to catch up with them. Hope returned to the previous crime scene and killed Lottie Taylor not far from his other victims. Seeing several women in a field nearby, he made a rush towards them. However, when they tried to escape, Hope pursued one of the women, Helena Belgrave, hacked her down, and then caught up with another, Louisina Walkes. He slashed and hacked her 22 times, killing her. It is alleged that when Hopey was about to target another person, someone shouted "Pretty, Hopey, pretty" and this distraction saved that person's life.

Afterwards, Hope, like a man possessed, followed several labourers to Bruce Vale River where he chanced upon Ella Bynoe, Rosa King, and John Richard Vaughn, who were preparing stones for road maintenance. He passed Vaughn and hit Bynoe twice on the head, but only with the broad side of the blade, allowing her to escape. King, still in shock at what had transpired asked, "Hopie, what the ...(expletive) you doing? You is a mad man or wha?" Without hesitation, Hope turned on King and in butcher like fashion, chopped her on the back of her neck, almost decapitating her.

The now out-of-control Hope, then exclaimed: "Is Clarke and he family I want." He then made his way towards Lakes Tenantry, where he saw a number of speculators buying pigs. He killed one pig, and while the people fled in terror, he killed a second pig and wounded a mule. Afterwards, he entered the home of a man named Springer, but finding no one inside, he smashed the interior. Next, he proceeded to Clarke's house, smashed the door in, and set fire to the dwelling. The flames were put out soon after he left.

Returning to Haggatts' yard, Seon saw two donkeys. He killed the first by puncturing its diaphragm, and injured the other severely, before moving further to the yard. There he tried to enter a factory, but was stopped at the door by the manager, Mr. Robinson, who pointed a gun at him and threatened to shoot him if he didn't leave the labourers alone.

Hope left and was soon stopped by Lance Corporal Mayers, who ordered him to put down his weapon. Since Mayers was armed with a revolver, Hope threw his machete into a cane field, where he was subdued and taken into custody.

Hope's rampage lasted for an hour, claiming four lives on the spot, and leaving six other people wounded. One of them, a woman, later died of her injuries.

At the preliminary enquiry, Seon Hope was charged with two counts of murder and was scheduled to be tried at the Court of Grand Sessions. There he was sentenced to death after a five-hour trial, where he stated: "Tell my father to take the calf."

According to the Barbados Weekly of May 15th, 1933 "the final curtain fell on the last act of the Haggatts tragic drama" the Tuesday morning of March 28th, 1933. It went on to say that Hope walked from a felon's cell to pay with his life for the lives of others. He was "hanged by the neck until he was dead" at Glendairy Prison and from the post mortem results, death was pronounced as being instantaneous.

Five people between the ages of 27 and 30 years old were killed that day and six wounded. Haggatts in St Andrew has long moved on. After all, it has been more than 80 years since this tragedy occurred. All of the persons who were around when this happened have since died. However, few have left the oral history to share through generations. Those who are in their 70s remember their parents telling them about "Sow Hope" and how he terrorised the district those many years ago. The young people that remain have absolutely no clue about that tragic day. One descendant of Hope was located, but he stated that Hope was the dark sheep of the family, who he only heard about less than ten years' prior from his grandfather – Hope's brother. Generally, Hope was not discussed, only in negative terms such as "wicked". He brought a stain to the family name, and like the community, they too have moved on.

What were the motives behind Hope's erratic behaviour? Were there warning signs? Did Hope reach a tipping point? Was Hope a sociopath? Regardless of the explanation, the case represented one of the worse possible outcomes of deviant behaviour at the time in Barbados. This led *The Barbados Weekly* of May 1933 to refer to the massacre as "unprecedented in the colony's history".

Happy Cot Murders (1983)

Fifty years after the Haggatts murders, the suburban community of Happy Cot in Bank Hall, St Michael suffered a similar fate. Happy Cot is a tiny community located in Mansion Road, which is found on the turnoff route from Station Hill to Abundant Life Assembly church.

On the morning of Tuesday, March 22nd, 1983, Ernest Greenidge went berserk and started attacking his neighbours with a butcher knife.

Ernest, who was 41 at the time, was described as a quiet person. According to journalist Heather-Lynn Evanson, not a bad word could have been said about him. He went about his business, always had a kind word for his neighbours and generally lived well with those in the community.

All that changed one eventful Tuesday morning when Ernest 'tripped'. The first sign that something was wrong came around 8:00 a.m. Fifty-year old Joseph Hinds was standing outside his home when Ernest, a small man compared to Hinds, approached him and asked: "You ever see me trouble anyone?"

"No," Hinds responded. This seemingly harmless response almost ended Hinds' life. Ernest took out a knife and stabbed Hinds in his abdomen, followed by another stab.

At around 8:10 a.m., 72-year-old Leslie Ifill and his 67-year-old wife, Madeline were the next victims of Ernest's wrath. The elderly couple was always together and as usual at that time of the morning, they were tending to plants in their garden. Sweat poured from their sun parched bodies as the weather was hot and humid. Mrs. Ifill went inside to fetch water for the two of them. No sooner than Mrs. Ifill went inside to get the glasses of water, her husband got a surprise visitor. He heard a familiar sounding voice and looked up to see Ernest walking in his direction without saying his usual greeting.

He asked Leslie "You know I ain't trouble nobody since I live here?"

"No son," Leslie replied, quickly followed by a question of his own. "Son, tell me who trouble you?"

There was no verbal response from Ernest. Instead, he turned his blood-stained knife on Mr Ifill, opening the elderly man's stomach. By then, Madeline returned to witness the horror unfolding. She too was greeted with a stab to the abdomen. The two glasses with water fell from her hands as she stumbled to the ground close to where her husband lay bleeding. A resident, who witnessed what happened and went to help Madeline, almost collapsed in fear as Ernest turned his eyes on her. She quickly aborted her plans and fled for her life.

On his way from Ifill's house, Greenidge pounced upon his neighbour Margaret Norris, 29, and stabbed her in the stomach.

But Ernest wasn't done yet. His next target was the Callender house. By the time he left the Callenders, three of the family members lay bleeding from knife wounds including Kenneth Callender and his wife Lillian.

Greenidge continued, unabated. When it was all over, nine people including three men, four women and two children had felt his wrath. The children were Meesha Webster, a three-year-old girl and an eight-year-old boy, Michael Callender, nephew of deceased Kenneth Callender. Michael was stabbed in the left side of his chest.

Colbert Callender, 35 years of age at the time, recalled the ordeal.

"Me and me neighbour came within inches of the knife blade, but escaped the fury of Greenidge. I heard a big shout and a man screaming 'Murder! Murder!' So I ran out and saw this gentleman running the other person around an old car with a knife in his hand. I did not know if he had been stabbed before. When I got to him,

I heard him say 'look he there' and when I got to the front of my family's house, I saw the man with a knife inside the house.

"As I was climbing the front steps, this same gentleman approached me and I ran. I collided with a fence, and he approached me and let go two stabs at me, and I ran faster and managed to get away. When I came back, I found that five members in my family had been stabbed and some other neighbours in the area."

A body builder from the area said "I did not run and he passed only inches from me, and looked straight in my face and said, 'I don't have any business with you'. He then walked right pass me."

According to **Nation** newspaper reports, a middle aged woman from Happy Cot said that on awakening early that morning, she did not feel well, so she told her daughter to call her workplace for her and report that she was ill.

She said "When I heard someone shout from another house and say that someone had gone mad, I called the police and told them to come quickly. They came as soon as I put down the phone."

She said she closed all the windows of the house, drew the curtains and told her daughter to keep quiet.

Meanwhile, Ernest had by then turned the knife on himself, slashing his chest and cutting his neck. When police arrived, they tried with difficulty to subdue him. He was rushed to the Queen Elizabeth Hospital, where like his victims, he was rushed to surgery. He survived, but some of his victims did not. The patriarch of the Callender family, Kenneth Callender, 70 years old, succumbed to his injuries despite going to surgery.

Margaret Norris, who had been rushed to the hospital about 8:30 a.m. died the next day after sustaining abdominal injuries. By the end of the month, Mr Leslie Ifill also succumbed to his injuries.

Two years later, in 1985, while on remand alternating between Glendairy Prison and the Psychiatric Unit, Ernest Greenidge, died at the Queen Elizabeth Hospital before he could be tried for the three murders. Neighbours said that he had died after not eating anything in prison.

Reflections

Residents of Happy Cot who resided in the community at the time, remembered the events of that fateful day with some persons suggesting some factors that could have contributed to Greenidge's behaviour that morning. One resident said that Greenidge had just lost his job at a company in Wildey in St Michael, and that set him off that morning. Another resident blamed it on a failed relationship. Whatever the reason, something triggered an otherwise quiet man, who clearly lost all coping mechanisms, to turn on his neighbours.

A middle-aged man from the community remembered that Greenidge took his neighbours by surprise. Recalling how Margaret lost her life, he said Greenidge had shouted her name while waiting like a predator for her to open her door. Quite unsuspectingly and innocently, Margaret went to the door and the moment she opened it, Greenidge sliced open her stomach with his knife.

The neighbour recalled that he did that with everyone he encountered. This neighbour luckily had already left for work, and heard about the incident while on the job. He recalled that he was allowed to leave work for the remainder of the day.

Like Haggatts and their tragedy in 1933, Happy Cot has also moved on. In fact, very few people talk about the incident of the day when one of their own turned on the community. The children who were injured are now adults who have their own children and they too have moved on. Happy Cot has been restored to living up to its name of peace and happiness.

CRIME SCENE DO NOT CROSS

CHAPTER TWO

Christmas Morning Murder at the Rectory

St Matthew's Rectory in 1967

Reverend Charles Gale and his wife Elizabeth left Canada and headed to Barbados in 1966, where Charles was to take up the five-year post of Vicar at the St Matthews Church. The couple was excited to be in Barbados, a welcome getaway from the chilly weather up north. Little did Reverend Gale know that a year later, his life would be turned upside down.

On Christmas eve night of 1967, Reverend Gale left the vicarage to conduct midnight mass at his church, leaving his heavily pregnant wife Elizabeth at home, with their three-year-old son Owen and their two-year-old daughter. Mrs Gale was expecting her third child in February of the next year.

On Christmas morning, December 25th, 1967, Barbadians woke up to the shocking news that Elizabeth Gale, the wife of the Vicar, as well as their son, Owen had been brutally murdered. According to reports, a shocked Reverend Gale, on returning home that morning, found his wife still in bed, but with her arms tied across her chest, and her head bound with clothing. He tried to loosen the clothing which bound her, and attempted to revive her, but to no avail. She died from asphyxia as a result of being smothered.

Gale reported to the police that he found their three-year-old son Owen bound and gagged. According to Gale, Elizabeth was barely alive and his son Owen was already dead. Mysteriously, the couple's two-year-old daughter was found unharmed and playing alone under the Christmas tree.

Mrs Gale was rushed to the Queen Elizabeth Hospital, arriving there around 2.25 a.m. but she was declared dead on arrival. The medical practitioner, later at the trial, declared that death had occurred within the preceding three hours.

The gruesome murders threw a damper on Christmas festivities throughout the island. Who could have wanted to harm the Gales? After all, they were quiet unassuming Christians whose only mission was to spread the Word of God. What could have possibly warranted someone taking the lives of not one, but three persons (one a baby in utero), in such a horrible fashion?

After the murders, Elizabeth's father called from Wales, where she was born, and spoke with the Dean, while Reverend Gale was staying at the home of the Archdeacon for a few days.

The next day, police arrested two men and charged them with the double murder of the wife of the Canadian Vicar of St Matthew's church and their three-year-old son.

St Matthew's Church today

The two men, Wingrove Brathwaite, 21 and Carlton McGlorie, 18 both of Browne's Gap, Hothersal Turning, appeared in court on December 27th for the murders. A large crowd of spectators thronged the courtyard to get a glimpse of the two labourers, as they entered the court under police arrest. No evidence was taken and Magistrate Errol Chase adjourned the preliminary hearing until January 3rd, 1968.

Wingrove Brathwaite, who was born to the late Effrey Brathwaite, attended St Matthew's Primary School, but never attended secondary school. Some residents of Hothersal Turning who knew Wingrove were divided in their views on his innocence or guilt. Some persons described him as quiet and expressed shock when they found out that he had been arrested and charged with the murders. On the contrary, the majority described him as 'wicked', 'not a nice person,' 'troublesome and very disobedient', among other unsavoury descriptions. One lady who grew up in the same community with Brathwaite said that she remembered him walking around naked as a teenager because his parents would take off his clothes to keep him from moving around or going outside, but he would still go outside naked.

McGlorie was a Dominican living with Brathwaite. One lady who also grew up with both men described McGlorie as "violent and would come up behind you with two stones and then knock you down with those two stones."

On December 30th, the Reverend Charles Gale left Barbados for his native Canada with his two-year-old daughter. On that same flight were the bodies of his wife and son.

Trial and retrial

Wingrove Brathwaite was tried alone for the murder of Elizabeth and Owen Gale. His accomplice, Carlton McGlorie turned Crown witness against Brathwaite and testified as the star witness in the case. Brathwaite was found guilty of murder, and sentenced to death. He appealed his death sentence. On his appeal, the conviction was quashed and a new trial ordered. On his retrial, he won an appeal on the conviction for the murder of Elizabeth Gale, but was again convicted of murdering Owen, her son.

The Appeal

According to the transcripts of the decision in the Appeal, the Crown's case was that the Appellant broke into the St Matthew's Vicarage for the purpose of stealing. Elizabeth Gale, the Vicar's wife, was in bed and the appellant bound her face with some articles of clothing and raped her. She died of asphyxia as a result of having her face tied. The principal witness for the Crown was McGlorie who had been charged jointly with the appellant for the offence, but in respect of whom the Crown entered a *nolle prosequi,* which is a dismissal of charges by the prosecution. This was most likely because he offered to testify against Brathwaite. However, McGlorie admitted in his evidence that he had lied in two previous statements made to the police. No reference was made to this admission in the summation of the trial.

One of these statements was "put in" on the application of the defence and disclosed a substantially different story from that to which McGlorie testified in court. This statement incorporated an alleged confession by the appellant to McGlorie that "he went to the place and 'had' the reverend wife."

On October 30th 1969, Justice Denys Williams sentenced Brathwaite to hang for the murder of Owen Gale. When asked if he had anything to say before the judge pronounced sentence, Brathwaite, who it was reported remained calm and collected throughout the trial, replied "I am innocent of this charge."

Justice Denys Williams donned his black cap and the court rose as the judge pronounced the death sentence.

Prior to the declaration of sentence, Brathwaite had made a statement from the dock in his defence the day prior. He said "As I have said before in my previous trials, about 10:30 pm on Christmas Eve night in 1967, I did not go to the vicarage with McGlorie or made any plans to do so.

"About 10:30 p.m. that same night, I left home and went to Hothersal Turning corner from where I got a lift in a car to the upper end of Roebuck Street just opposite the Globe Theatre. I do not know the name of the driver or the number of the car.

"I left the Globe and went into Queen's Park. When the dance started, I listened to the music and then went into the Steel Shed where I played cards with some other boys.

"McGlorie had left me at home and the first time I had seen him since that time was when he joined the game in the shed about 2:30 a.m. Sometime after 5:00 a.m., Christmas morning, I gave Junior Howell 75 cents for a cigarette lighter in the presence of McGlorie and I left Queen's Park about 6:00 am Christmas morning," he said.

Senior Crown Counsel, Lindsay Worrell, in his address to the jury, which lasted for about 43 minutes, said that Brathwaite, through a deliberate and wicked act, caused death to Owen Frederick Gale.

"The issues are quite clear," he said "and when you consider all the evidence, there is only one conclusion which you can come to, and that is that the accused, Wingrove Brathwaite, deliberately and cruelly killed little Owen Gale."

Deighton Rawlins, in his one-hour address, told the jury that the star witness for the prosecution, Carlton McGlorie, was a blatant liar and an accomplice. He said that there was no evidence in the case to support that more than one person went to the vicarage that night.

"The only evidence of importance is that of Carlton McGlorie, and it is only an attempt on his part to save his own neck," Mr Rawlins stressed.

Justice Denys Williams told the jury that from McGlorie's story, it was obvious that he and the accused were at the vicarage the night of the murders.

He then cautioned them of accepting McGlorie's evidence by telling them that it was dangerous to act on his evidence, unless it was corroborated. The judge advised the jury that there was no evidence in the case capable of amounting to corroboration.

"However," he said, "you must act on his testimony, but you must approach it with caution."

The jury however, believed McGlorie and found Wingrove Brathwaite guilty of murder.

According to the transcript in the decision in the Appeal, "The important fact of the matter here is that the case for the Crown was based in substance on the evidence of Carlton McGlorie, who was with Wingrove Brathwaite that night. The Appeals Court admitted that without his evidence, the charge could not be established against the appellant. McGlorie had originally been charged jointly with Brathwaite for the crime, but had been discharged on a *nolle prosequi* being entered. At the trial he testified that he and Brathwaite entered the vicarage that night for the purpose of stealing. Brathwaite went upstairs and he remained downstairs. He (McGlorie) heard a tumbling on the floor from upstairs, went upstairs himself and entered a room where he saw Brathwaite holding a woman by her throat and squeezing her. The woman's legs were shaking on the bed and then the shaking ceased. McGlorie testified that he asked Brathwaite what all this was for and Brathwaite told him that the woman had seen him. They then proceeded from the room. He went downstairs thinking that Brathwaite was following. When Brathwaite did not come, he returned upstairs, re-entered the room where he had seen the woman and claimed that he saw Brathwaite on the woman. Brathwaite jumped from the bed saying that McGlorie had frightened him. According to McGlorie, Brathwaite's pants were down and his penis erect. The woman's hands were tied behind her neck and her face was tied.

McGlorie testified that Brathwaite stated that he had had intercourse with the woman and invited McGlorie to do likewise. McGlorie protested that he was not there for that purpose and refused. They then left the vicarage after Brathwaite had taken the wallet which was on a table downstairs.

Brathwaite appealed once again, challenging his conviction. Brathwaite denied killing Owen Gale, and appealed that the verdict was unreasonable having regard to the evidence. The only substantial evidence connecting the accused with the crime was that of the witness McGlorie, who it must be pointed out, admitted in evidence that he had lied in previous statements made to the police. However, the Appeals Court ruled that they could not brand the verdict of a jury as unreasonable merely because it was based substantially on the evidence of one witness.

The Court opined that if that witness was an accomplice or had or may have had an interest of his own to serve and there was some breach of recognised practice in the summation, that was another matter. Likewise, the Court argued, it was a different matter if adequate guidance was not given to the jury as to the manner in which they should approach the evidence of a witness who admitted having told lies in a previous contradictory statement. But for the appellant to succeed on the ground now being considered he must show that on an analysis of the evidence the verdict was unreasonable. The Appeals Court argued that in their view, the appellant had not been able to do this.

A further ground of appeal argued on behalf of Brathwaite was that the defence was not adequately put to the jury. It was said that the jury was never told that the defence of the accused was an alibi. The relevant part of the statement was as follows:

> 'On 24th December 1967 about ten to half past ten that night, I leave home and went to Hothersal Turning corner. I got a ride from there as far as the Globe, a car that I didn't know the driver or the number of the car. I leave the Globe when I got a drop down and went in the park. I listen a while to the music after the dance was started until about 2.00 am in the morning. Then I went and join a Romey game in the shed. After that Carlton came and join in the game... I never had any conversation with Carlton before leaving home about going any place for money. I never had any conversation with him in the park concerning the vicarage. Neither was I at the vicarage that night in question or throughout the period of Father Gale's residence there.'

The Appeals court, in their judgement opined:

> "We have considered whether we ought to order a retrial of the appellant on this charge. This is the second occasion on which the appellant was tried and convicted for this offence. On the first occasion a retrial was ordered. We are doubtful that the interests of justice require that another trial be ordered."

Wingrove Brathwaite was convicted on October 30th, 1969 for the murder of Owen Frederick Gale, three years old.

The trial judge in his summing-up left the issue of accomplice to the jury. He told them that if they found that McGlorie was an accomplice, it would be unsafe to convict him in the absence of corroboration. He also told them should they find that he was not an accomplice, they should treat his evidence as they would the evidence of any other witness.

Wingrove Brathwaite was convicted and sentenced to death. On August 20th, 1971, he was executed at Glendairy Prison for the murder of Owen Gale, son of the Reverend Charles Gale, of the vicarage on Christmas Day, 1967.

A few years after Brathwaite's execution, conspiracy theories emerged regarding the outcome of the case. First, it was rumoured that Reverend Charles Gale had committed a murder in Canada and had also confessed to the murder of his wife and son. However, the rumours were denied after contacts with the Reverend by the local media proved the allegations were false (Investigator, Friday, October 5th, 1990, p 19).

Second, persons in the community who believed Brathwaite was innocent said they believe that race was a factor in Brathwaite's execution because the victims were white. In addition, because nothing like that had ever happened in Barbados before, and because of Brathwaite's reputation, their were those who believed he did it.

There were also allegations that Brathwaite was beaten into a confession, but this also could obviously not be verified.

Discussions with retired crime sleuth Keith Whittaker and former Commissioner of Police also dismissed the story of the Reverend confessing to the murder of his wife. Whittaker was adamant that the police conducted thorough investigations into the murder and had significant evidence, including an eyewitness who was a nurse from the area who saw both Brathwaite and McGlorie entering the rectory that night. Whittaker, who said he worked on the case, said that Brathwaite confessed to the murders and had killed the little boy because the boy recognised him.

Orville Durant said in a telephone interview regarding the Wingrove Brathwaite case, "everything went smoothly. By midday the following day, everything was wrapped up. Our investigation immediately picked up Wingrove Brathwaite who was involved in this crime. He offered no resistance when arrested."

Regarding the story of the reverend's confession, Durant simply said "in every murder, there are rumours". He believed strongly, like Whittaker, that the right man was convicted and executed for the murders of the Gale family that fateful Christmas morning.

As for McGlorie, it is unclear as to whatever became of him. It was alleged that he lives somewhere in the island, but this could not be substantiated.

CRIME SCENE DO NOT CROSS

CHAPTER THREE

Who Killed *Pele*?
(Part 1)

"Not me and dah 'Pele' case bozie!"

T his is a common Bajan catch phrase used by the young and not so young at heart, which basically means "I am not getting involved in that story/situation." Many persons use this phrase, but only a few know where it came from. What is the mystery surrounding the *'Pele'* case which has resulted in this phrase which has transcended at least three generations?

Interestingly, the term "*not me and dah 'Pele' case bozie*" is the hook line in a calypso song called **The 'Pele' Case**, written by the late Sir Don Marshall, which was about the unsolved murder of Victor *'Pele'* Parris,

Victor 'Pele' Parris

who was shot in 1978 in Atlantic Shores, Christ Church. Below is an excerpt of the song.

> *I ain't know who is who, who statement false from true*
> *And how dem police do dey duty*
> *De whole thing seems to me, like some mystery movie*
> *We see pun CBC TV*
> *Not me and dah 'Pele' case bozie.*

On May 16th 1978, the quiet of Atlantic Shores, an upscale community on the south of the island, was shattered with the sound of gun fire.

When the gun smoke cleared, a man was dead, and a scandal that rocked Barbados for decades was born. That man was Victor *'Pele'* Parris, 30 years old at the time of his murder. His companion, who was with him when he was killed, Hyacinth Goring, remains the subject of scandal and rumour, fueled in part by her silence and lack of cooperation with the Commission of Enquiry that had been set up to investigate the murder. Miss Goring left Barbados at the time of the case.

This is the story of the *'Pele'* case, which continues to fascinate Barbadians some 41 years after it occurred.

To this day, no one has been charged with his murder.

Who was Victor 'Pele' Parris?

(Adapted from the Nation newspaper November 17, 1978)

Victor Desmond *'Pele'* Parris was born on September 19th, 1948 in My Lord's Hill, St Michael. He was the second child of six, and the first son born to Egbert Parris and his late wife, Elaine.

'Pele' was a healthy and affable child from birth. In his early years, he moved from My Lord's Hill and took up residence in Mount Friendship, St Barnabas, St Michael where he lived until the day of his death.

He attended the St Barnabas Boys' School and later at the age of nine years old, he entered Combermere School. He was considered a keen and dedicated student and was very involved in both his school and his community. At school, *'Pele'* played cricket and football and was actively involved in cultural and youth groups; church affairs and entertainment.

'Pele' was a sports-loving youth and it was because of his admiration for the Brazilian footballer, *'Pele'*, that he got his nickname.

Former school colleagues remember that it was *'Pele'* who was always the centre of attention on the school bus. He was remembered by a former school mate as "friendly with everybody, he mixed with everybody, and he never kept any bad feelings in mind for anybody."

During his school years and after leaving Combermere where he gained "O" Level passes in Engineering and Mathematics, he was actively involved in community groups such as West Ham, Regent Hill Youth and Cultural Group, Mapp Hill Sports Club, St Barnabas Sports Club; Combermere Old Scholars' Association, Haggatt Hall Sports Club and others.

One Pinelands friend described *'Pele'* in the following way:

"He spread himself like one hundred men throughout the whole community and everybody loved and respected him."

Victor Parris was also a Sunday School teacher and very active in the St Barnabas Church. At the time of his death, he was the coordinator and Public Relations Officer with the Pinelands Youth Group.

Recalling his ambitions as a teenager, his father said *'Pele'* expressed the desire to be an engineer. From Combermere, he took his first job in the engineering section of the Ministry of Communications and Works (MCW) as a lather.

During the three years he spent there, he also took out a correspondence course in Civil Engineering from an overseas college.

After his stint at MCW, he found himself entering an unexpected field. He took up an appointment as a teacher at Kaye's Academy in Chelsea Road and remained there for almost three years during which time he acted as headmaster for about a year.

Soon after, he became active in another field - politics.

The 1976 general election in Barbados was a historical turning point in Barbadian politics. The Barbados Labour Party was swept into power with a landslide 17 to 7 seat majority. Among those toasting the victory was Victor *'Pele'* Parris.

His father Egbert recalls that for *'Pele'*, this triumph was also a personal triumph. He said, "He went all out during the campaign; and there is no one who can say that he did not play a decisive role in that victory."

"He had also become a member of the Barbados Labour Party and was at one-time secretary of the constituency branch. He even told me at one time that he had been promised a post on the executive of the party," his father recalled.

His father continued, "I remembered him saying at one time that he liked the party and that he would see the 1976 general elections through and then quit politics."

It was about eight months before his death that *'Pele'* entered yet another field when he left Kaye's Academy to take up an appointment at Welcome Inn Hotel in the Accounts section. He eventually became the Financial Controller.

His ambition was to become a qualified accountant and he had started making his own preparations. He enrolled with the Barbados Institute of Management and Productivity (BIMAP) in 1975, paying his way out of his pocket. He was successful in all the courses he took between 1975 and 1977 at BIMAP.

Victor's aim was to go to the United States to enroll in a university to study for a degree, a dream he was never to realise.

This medium-height, slim, energetic sports-loving, party-going, fun-loving, charismatic *'Pele'* was very popular with the girls and had a varied love life.

His father said he had many girlfriends during his lifetime, but the last one he expressed any real feelings for to him was Hyacinth Goring, the girl who was with him on the evening of his death.

Mr Parris said, "I believe it was about three or four months that the two of them were seeing each other, and on more than one occasion, he told me that he really liked her.

"He had no car of his own, so I would take him to work on mornings, and she would bring him home at night. It might sound strange, but I never got the chance to meet her, and in fact, the first time I saw her was in court during the hearing.

"I remember one night after she dropped him off, he came into the house and found me still up and told me, 'If I knew you were still awake, I would have introduced you to my girlfriend'."

The elder Parris said that *'Pele'* talked to him about his affection for Hyacinth frequently.

"I even remember once warning him to be careful and he told me that was no problem.

His father said that during the last days of his life, *'Pele'* had never told him of any problems or fears he was experiencing.

He however noted that when he visited the mortuary to view the body the day after the death, he overheard one of the people there say that *'Pele'* had said that somebody had threatened his life and had been looking for him with a gun.

A close friend said that *'Pele'* had begun showing signs of fear and stress before his death, but had never told him what the problem was.

At 8:55 a.m. on May 17th, Egbert Parris dropped his son to work as usual, never suspecting that would be the last time he would see him alive. That same night, *'Pele'* joined his mother, who died when he was just 14 years old.

Coroner's Inquest leads to Commission of Enquiry

A lengthy coroner's inquest which commenced in October 1978, was filled with drama and suspense, and then Coroner of the District 'A' Court, Keith Simmons concluded the inquest with his belief that Parris was murdered, that witnesses had lied to him (the coroner) under oath, and that a member of the Royal Barbados Police Force was indifferent to the case.

The Coroner said that although there is evidence that *'Pele'* was murdered, neither a certain policeman, nor important witnesses, played their part in the interest of truth.

Mr Simmons said that "in the circumstances, I am going to give an open verdict".

The **Nation** newspaper said at the time in their front page editorial titled *'Make an Arrest'* dated October 11th, 1978 that they would not rest until prompt action was taken to bring the murderer to justice, nor did they wish that the matter would become another statistic in the Criminal Records Department of the Royal Barbados Police Force.

In the front page editorial, the **Nation** thought it important to bring two major matters to the fore. One was what Mr Simmons said in relation to the evidence of some of the witnesses and in particular that of Miss Hyacinth Goring, who was with the victim at the time of his death. The second dealt with the attitude of a police-man in the course of giving evidence before the coroner's court.

The magistrate said in relation to the first matter, "This court has found it extremely difficult to believe the evidence of some of the more important witnesses, and in particular Miss Hyacinth Goring who it would appear finds it extremely difficult to tell the truth. It is in this regard that I am forced to comment on the investigations carried out in this case."

In the second matter of concern, Mr Simmons said, "We in Barbados are accus-tomed to a high standard of policing, but it is regrettable to state that in many respects, this high standard to which we are accustomed, fell to a new low."

He added "at one stage there was some degree of indifference on the part of a policeman in giving his evidence."

While acknowledging that the RBPF was a good police force, the **Nation** editorial said that their failure in the *'Pele'* case was a glaring example that was too dangerous to be tolerated.

It also called for the removal of any policeman who fell below that high standard from the ranks of the Royal Barbados Police Force as a public demonstration of commitment to the integrity of service in the enforcement of law.

They demanded to know who killed Victor *'Pele'* Parris and believed that the answer laid in a thorough investigation "to be initiated immediately". The **Nation** called for Scotland Yard or its equal to come in to Barbados to find out who killed *'Pele'* "not only in the interest of his family in St Barnabas, but on behalf of all Barbadians who believe in the sanctity of life".

The Commission of Enquiry into *'Pele's* murder

The Barbados Labour Party set up a Commission of Enquiry called the Malone Commission to investigate the Parris murder.

The Commission was headed by a West Indian High Court Judge, Sir Denis Malone (chairman), along with Commander James Nevill of Britain's Scotland Yard and Superintendent Bruce Northrop of the Royal Canadian Mounted Police (RCMP).

Below are the facts of the case along with an edited version of the Enquiry into Victor *"Pele"* Parris' death.

On the afternoon of May 16th, 1978, around 4:00 p.m., on leaving the Hastings branch of the Royal Bank of Canada where she was employed as a typist clerk, Hyacinth Goring told her fellow employee, Beverly, that she was going to pick up "P", visit a hairdressing salon, and then go with her boyfriend Victor *'Pele'* Parris, to Atlantic Shores to allegedly look at land. "P," as Beverly explained, was the nickname by which Hyacinth Goring referred to Victor Parris. It was also revealed by Valerie, who ran a hairdressing salon called 'Val's Hairway' in the Regency Cove Hotel, that Hyacinth Goring requested Margaret, Valerie's assistant, to call the Welcome Inn, where Parris worked and tell *'Pele'* that she would be late. The reason she was late was never revealed.

About 8:00 p.m., Angus Edghill, who lived on a bluff overlooking the Atlantic Shores coast road, was at home in his garden when he heard two shots followed by screams. Some seconds later, he saw a figure running down the coast road towards a car which was travelling from the west.

Around the same time, Mr E. McComie, in whose company was Miss H. Williams, was driving his car along the Atlantic Shores coast road. McComie and Williams said that just after they turned into the particular section, immediately before driving up a small incline, a car with headlamps on full beam passed them, going in a westerly direction. Parked in the cul-de-sac he saw a car, G 29, and seconds before he saw the young woman, a car passed him travelling at a fast rate. He did not recognise that car and it has never been traced.

Miss Williams said the car was white or cream in colour, but Mr McComie said he was momentarily blinded by the glare of the car's headlamps and couldn't tell the colour of the car, only that it had two headlamps and not four.

They both said that seconds after the car passed they heard a scream. Their car travelled another 20 yards and they heard a second scream.

At that point, they saw a woman running towards them in the glare of their headlights and she began shouting and screaming. Miss Williams said that the woman was clad only in a pair of panties and a blouse, but Mr McComie said he could only see she was wearing panties and observed nothing else.

According to reports, the young woman was Hyacinth Goring and she was dressed in a blouse and panty. She reported that whilst with her boyfriend in G29, an unknown man had appeared. He shot her boyfriend and indicated he wanted to have sex with her but she had escaped.

Mr McComie said he became alarmed, and put his car into reverse, but the woman ran up to them and cried, 'Cud dear, don't leave me up here."

He asked her what was the matter, and she said a man had just been shot and he (the man who did the shooting) was trying to rape her.

Mr McComie then told her to get into the car, and he turned around to drive the way back.

Without any further questioning from Mr McComie or Miss Williams, Miss Goring related how she and her boyfriend had gone into the area to look at some land.

She told them that while they (she and Victor) were sitting in the car talking, a man came up and tried to have sex with her. Her boyfriend tried to prevent the stranger's assault, and the man countered by shooting *'Pele'* in the arm.

According to Hyacinth, *'Pele'* tried to protect her. She told them they could not leave Parris up there, and pleaded with them to go to the aid of her fallen lover, telling them that all her things – without specifying them - were still in the parked car.

According to Heather Williams, Hyacinth Goring spoke to the gunman as "now" trying to rape her. She also appeared scared and only moments before reaching Mr McComie's car, her screams had been heard by Mr Edghill. Yet, she wanted to go back to the car G29, as soon as she was in Mr McComie's car. The Enquiry report stated that it was surprising that she would want to go back to the car, if (as she alleged) she had just escaped from a gunman and the threat of rape, when she had given no indication that she knew the gunman and potential rapist to be no longer there. The Commission also queried whether concern for a lover would overcome the natural reluctance of a young woman to return to a dark and lonely place where she did not know if the man who had just tried to rape her was still lurking around the area and who she knew was armed with a gun which he had used to shoot her lover. Perhaps likely, they said. However, unlikely that in those circumstances, a young woman would express a wish to return to such a place because her "things" were there, even supposing that amongst those things was, according to Hyacinth, a sum of money as large as $1,100.00.

She asked to go back to G29. Mr McComie refused. Instead, he offered to take her to the police station, but she declined the offer, insistent that she could not go to the station dressed as she was.

Mr McComie said he was not going back there because he feared the man with the gun might still be around, and immediately left the scene for the nearest police station. It was at this point, he said that Miss Goring pointed out that she could not go to the police station because her father was a former police sergeant, and if he saw her in that condition, he would kill her.

He permitted her to get into the back seat of his car when he was about 200 yards west of the cul-de-sac at the eastern end of the Atlantic Shores coast road.

Hyacinth's first stop – the Smith residence

She then asked to be taken to the home of a friend, Mr S. Smith, who lived in Enterprise Gardens, so she could get someone to put in a phone call to the police later.

The couple said that they didn't have to drive far to where the woman wanted to go, but it was through a lot of "twisting and turning" and took about two and a half minutes to reach there.

Police at the scene of the murder in Atlantic Shores

At the house, Miss Goring asked Mr McComie to blow his horn to get the attention of someone inside the house, which he did, but no one came out.

Miss Williams said she noticed a light in the kitchen window and saw someone looking out, but eventually Miss Goring had to get out of the car and walk up to the front door. The couple drove away immediately and did not see who had answered the woman.

Mr Smith said he was having supper when Hyacinth Goring arrived at his home. He had known her when he once lived in Workmans, St George, which is where Hyacinth Goring was living with her parents, but he did not recognise her immediately. He said that Hyacinth

Hyacinth Goring

ran from the car which had just dropped her off, screaming his first name, but although he had let her into his house, he told the Commission he had not recognised her until 30 minutes later, when she mentioned the name of her boyfriend, Mr Lee, who was also known to the Smiths. (The Commission of Enquiry later discredited this story, because Mr Smith admitted that he had lived in the same neighbourhood as the Goring family, had known Hyacinth then, and that she had visited him in Atlantic Shores up to the year before).

Also present at Mr Smith's home when Hyacinth Goring arrived, was his wife, Mrs P. Smith. Unlike her husband, she recognised Hyacinth Goring at once and claimed that she tried to dissuade her husband from allowing Miss Goring to enter the house, but her husband "disobeyed" her.

While Mr Smith was eating his supper and his wife watched television, Hyacinth Goring recounted her story of an attack by an unknown gunman, and in doing so, mentioned that she had offered the gunman money and that she wanted to go back to her car. Mr Smith told the Commission that after he heard Miss Goring's story, he continued eating his dinner, and decided that he would go with her to the scene of the shooting after he had eaten and changed his clothes.

Mrs Smith told the Commission that although it seemed to her that Miss Goring was in serious trouble, she (Mrs Smith) continued to watch television.

"Are you asking us seriously to believe that?" Sir Denis asked.

"I said I continued to watch television," the witness repeated.

Asked by the Commission chairman whether she had no feeling for her fellow human being, Mrs Smith retorted: "What was I supposed to do?"

Mrs Smith also said that she had no idea why Miss Goring had visited her house that night. "She made no mention of assistance or medical attention for the man," she stated.

Regarding Miss Goring's condition, Mrs Smith said Hyacinth's hair was in a disorderly manner, and the blouse she was wearing was dirty on the lower front.

Asked whether she meant dirt from the earth, the witness curtly replied, "Dirty."

She later described it as mud, and when the Commission referred to an earlier statement by the same witness, Mrs Smith agreed there were blood stains on Miss Goring's blouse.

It was revealed that Miss Goring's clothes were cleaned and ironed, and she had a bath before leaving the Smith's residence. Mrs Smith said this happened after the police had visited the crime scene and had taken away Parris.

She said that when Miss Goring came to their home, half naked shouting for her husband, she told him not to open the door. "I am not accustomed to that drama. He disobeyed me and opened the door. That's why I am here today," Mrs Smith declared.

She told the Commission she did not know who Victor (Parris) was; that Miss Goring did not tell her that she had left $1,100.00 in her handbag at the murder scene, and that she did not at the time know Miss Goring's father was a policeman.

Commissioner Northrop asked Mrs Smith, "Didn't you find it strange that she wanted to go back to the scene right in the middle of things, with a gunman on the loose?"

Mrs Smith replied, "I got the impression she wanted to go back to collect her things. She laid emphasis on collecting her things."

Despite her lack of interest in the report, Smith admitted supplying Hyacinth with a pair of towelling shorts, and allowing her husband to use her car to take Miss Goring back to the murder scene.

She also admitted telephoning Miss Goring's mother, and under persistent questioning in which reference was drawn to her testimony at the coroner's inquest, Mrs Smith admitted she had helped to iron the blouse which her husband assisted Miss Goring in cleaning.

The Commissioners in the Enquiry surmised that the reason Hyacinth took a bath and cleaned the blouse by the Smiths that night was to get rid of incriminating evidence. Hyacinth never gave a reason for taking a bath.

Hyacinth's second stop – the crime scene

Mr Smith said that he changed his clothes, telephoned the police, and left in his wife's car MC613 with Hyacinth Goring for the scene. On arrival there, he found it so dark and dismal, that he did not get out of his car or allow Hyacinth to leave it. Instead, he drove from the scene to the house of Fitzroy Jackman with Hyacinth who was then dressed in shorts borrowed from Mrs Smith.

Hyacinth's third stop – the Jackman's residence

Mr Jackman's house faced the Atlantic Shores coast road. Visiting his home that night was Mrs Wendy Punnett-Hope. She was present with Mr Jackman when Mr Smith and Hyacinth arrived at Mr Jackman's house.

Mr Jackman and Mrs Hope testified that they were puzzled by the visit of Mr Smith and Hyacinth Goring and initially believed they were potential intruders. In fact, Mrs Hope said she was terrified because she felt Mr Smith and Miss Goring were trying to use a sad story to gain entry into Mr Jackman's home.

They were also puzzled because they could not understand the cause for the visit. When they heard Hyacinth Goring's story, they suggested to call an ambulance, but they were told that *'Pele'* was dead. When they offered to telephone the police, they were told that the police had been informed, and she was now on her way to the police station. Hyacinth then relayed the story about her father being a former policeman and that she worked at the Royal Bank and she could not go to the police station in that state. Mrs Hope added, "I didn't get the impression this was a woman whose friend had just been shot." Hope also told Hyacinth that she should allow nothing to detain her.

At the Enquiry, Mrs Hope told the Commission that Miss Goring was dressed in a cream or "off white" panty, her hair was short and combed back, she was barefooted, and Hyacinth, without prompting from either Jackman or Hope, revealed that she had already had a bath at the Smith's home before coming to their home.

But Fitzroy Jackman, who had seen Miss Goring after her first return trip to the scene, before the police actually arrived, told the Commission she was wearing a clean blouse.

"The young lady said she had a bath before coming to my house, I am sure of that", Jackman told the Commission.

That statement directly contradicted what Mrs Smith had said to the Commission prior. Mrs Smith had told the Enquiry that despite what Jackman had reported, she was adamant that Hyacinth Goring had bathed at her place, not on the first unannounced visit, but on the return trip from the murder scene, the same night Victor Parris was shot. This is discussed further in the chapter.

Regarding the two visitors to the Jackman's house, Mrs Hope told the Commission "Certainly what they were saying and how they were behaving did not coincide. She (Miss Goring) was explaining, but not hysterical. Mr Smith was very calm."

According to the Commission of Enquiry, what was confusing, was that Hyacinth Goring declared *'Pele'* as dead, even though Constable Mason, who later arrived on the scene of the murder with Sergeant Callender, said that when they arrived, they saw a man lying in the back of the car with his legs hanging out and he was groaning. Mason said it did not cross his mind to think why the woman said the man was dead, when he had heard him groaning, nor to ask her how she knew he was dead.

Miss Goring told the story of going to Atlantic Shores to look at land, and of being attacked by a man who ordered her to strip, and then shot Parris and escaped.

"But she never mentioned anything about a robbery, and nothing of rape, except by implication," said Mrs Hope. "She did not even attempt a description of the attacker."

When Mr Smith and Hyacinth left, Mr Jackman called the Oistins Police Station and was told that a report had already been made. However, the Enquiry was told that there was no record of Mr Jackman's phone call to the police station.

From the home of Mr Jackman, Mr Smith said that he was driving towards his home or towards Oistins, when he saw the police car with Sergeant David Callender and Police Constable Mason in it. He led them to the scene. There, he held a light whilst Sergeant Callender and PC Mason who found Victor Parris lying face down in the well between the front and back seats of G29, lifted him from the car and put him in the police car. Victor Parris was alive but unconscious. They rushed him to the Queen Elizabeth Hospital.

There were discrepancies with Mr Smith's testimony. First, he had said that the first time he called the police was on his return to the house with Hyacinth from the scene of the murder. Then he said he was not sure if he had called them before he left his house. At the Inquest which was held prior, Smith had said that when he left Mr Jackman's house, he was on his way home to call the police because Mrs Wendy Punnett-Hope had advised him to do so.

At the Enquiry, when he gave evidence, he blamed his inconsistencies on "faulty memory" and said that he had not gone back to his home after leaving the house of Mr Jackman and before meeting the police. Smith had earlier said that he was at home and saw the headlights of an approaching car and going out into the street to flag it down, but this he said was not the case. The Enquiry concluded that based on timelines, Smith would have telephoned the police after visiting the house of Mr Jackman, so Smith was untruthful in saying that he did not go back to his house because he met the police on his way to Oistins Police Station.

At the Queen Elizabeth Hospital

At about 9:00 pm. Sister Maria Babb and the day team of nurses in the Casualty Ward of the Queen Elizabeth Hospital were about to go off duty when Victor Parris was brought into the hospital so the nurses of both the day and night teams attended to him. On first arrival at the hospital, Victor Parris, according to some of the nurses, did not appear to be in a serious condition, and some of the nurses were not even aware that he had been shot.

Staff Nurse Janet Smith, who came on duty at 9:00 p.m. shortly after Victor had been taken to the Treatment Room of the Casualty Ward, recalled that he spoke the name "Hyacinth" more than once. All of the nurses reported that when Victor Parris was conscious he called the name "Hyacinth". He gave no account of how he came to be injured, but gave the name of Hyacinth as that of his next of kin. Shortly before he went into the coma, which ended with his death, he was reported by Nursing Assistant Joycelyn Stoute to have said that he wanted to take his shoes off. However, '*Pele*' was lying on the bed in his socks and without his shoes.

Two men came with him and one was recognised by some of the nurses to be Sergeant Callender.

At the Enquiry, some of the nurses said that while '*Pele*' spoke, the two men who had brought him into the hospital were close to the bed trolley on which he lay. However, both Sergeant Callender and P.C. Mason stated that Victor Parris appeared to them to be unconscious and that he did not speak.

After he had been in the Casualty Ward for about 15 minutes, Victor Parris became restless and it was feared that his condition was serious. He was taken to the X-Ray Room and from there to the Recovery Room. In the Recovery Room, Assistant Nurse Stoute heard him request the removal of his shoes and to be assisted to sit up. He was then lying on a bed. An operation was performed to insert a tube to drain the blood collected in his body from internal haemorrhaging. He went into a coma and died at 10:44 p.m.

Hyacinth's fourth stop – the Smith residence (again)

Meanwhile, back in Atlantic Shores, after Sergeant Callender and PC Mason had taken Victor Parris to the hospital, Mr Smith and Hyacinth returned to Mr Smith's house. Hyacinth then changed from the shorts she had borrowed from Mrs Smith into the skirt which according to Mr Smith, she had taken from G29, while Sergeant Callender and P.C. Mason were removing Victor from the car.

Testimony of Sergeant Kenneth Legall

Sergeant Kenneth Legall testified that he was at Oistins Police Station the night of May 16th, 1978 and was about to go off duty when he heard the report of the shooting at Atlantic Shores, and as Sergeant in charge of the station, put off his leave and followed his detective Corporal David Callender who was first to reach the scene of the murder.

At about 8:50 p.m., Sergeant Legall arrived at the home of Mr Smith. Hyacinth Goring, he said, told him of a gunman who had shot Victor Parris. Sergeant Legall said that he telephoned the hospital and spoke to Sergeant Callender who told him that Inspector Byron Clarke, his senior, had given instructions that Sergeant Legall was not to go to the scene but to await his (Clarke's) arrival.

He said he met Miss Goring at the home of Scofield Smith after rambling in Atlantic Shores without locating the murder scene and heard her story for the first time.

Legall revealed that when he got to the Smith's home, Miss Goring was in a room talking with Mrs Smith and when she (Miss Goring) came out, she was fully clothed, her hair was in order, and according to him, "she was quite calm." She was also dressed in her full uniform of skirt and blouse. (Bear in mind that Hyacinth had said to Sergeant Callender that the shooter took her skirt, and then later she took the same skirt from the car at the scene the first time she returned).

According to Sergeant Legall, Hyacinth reported that just as they had arrived at Atlantic Shores, and got out of the car, a man came up to them, holding something bright in his hand, and told her to take off her clothes.

As it related to Miss Goring's statement to Legall, 'Pele' asked the man why he didn't leave them alone. She (Hyacinth) then asked the man if she took off her clothes if he would leave them alone, and when he answered yes, she slipped back into the car from the driver's side.

Hyacinth Goring told Sergeant Kenneth Legall that the gunman at Atlantic Shores ordered her to strip, but it was Victor "Pele" Parris who obeyed the instructions and started to undress before he was shot by the assailant.

The story went on, "Parris was outside and started to unbutton his shirt. Just as Parris was unbuttoning his shirt, the man fired two shots, and she saw Parris fall to the ground.

"The man ran away. She (Miss Goring) tried lifting Parris back into the car, but he was too heavy and she left him and ran and shouted for help."

The police sergeant told the Commission although Miss Goring had not mentioned to him what time she and Parris got to Atlantic Shores, he was of the opinion that the attack had taken place in the dark, and although he found it strange that they would have gone to look at land in the dark, he did not question Miss Goring about it then.

"I was slightly doubtful she was telling the truth, and when I got to the scene, I was really doubtful," Sergeant Legall said.

Sergeant Legall added that Miss Goring did not tell him her attacker was disguised. She made no mention of the man demanding money; she told him nothing about $1100.00 and he could not recall asking her why Parris started to undress, after the gunman ordered her to strip.

Legall testified that even though he saw Hyacinth fully dressed, Mr Smith whispered to him as he was leaving "Don't mind how that girl is dressed, she actually came here in a bare pair of panties."

Inspector Bryon Clarke was at choir practice when Victor Parris arrived at the hospital. Sergeant Callender said that he went to St. Mary's church where Inspector Clarke was, and from there, after stopping at Central Police Headquarters, they went to the hospital. At the hospital, Inspector Clarke claimed that he went to the Recovery Room to see Victor Parris and to arrange for the taking of a dying declaration by P.C. Mason. The hospital staff said that Clarke did not.

Dr Brathwaite, who performed the autopsy on Victor Parris, said in his opinion, Victor's life could have been saved if he had received medical attention earlier than he did.

CRIME SCENE DO NOT CROS

CHAPTER FOUR
Who Killed *Pele*? (Part 2)

F rom the hospital, Inspector Clarke and Sergeant Callender said they drove to Oistins. At the foot of Oistins Hill, they met PC Merritt driving his Austin 1100 car.

Victor 'Pele' Parris

PC Merritt was off duty at the time and on the instruction of Inspector Clarke, left his car in the yard of Oistins Police Station, got into the police Rover car, M3107, and drove with Inspector Clarke and Sergeant Callender first to the neighbourhood of the house of Mr Smith and then to the crime scene.

Simultaneously, Hyacinth's mother received a call from the Smiths, passing on instructions from Hyacinth to get in touch with her boyfriend, Mr Lee and ask him to go over to Mr Smith's house to meet her (Hyacinth). The mother tried to find out what was wrong, but the caller would not say.

Later, Hyacinth's sister made repeated calls to the Smith's residence and "when we asked to speak to Hyacinth, we heard she was not available and those sorts of things", the older sister testified at the Commission of Enquiry.

Mr Lee was not at home when Marguerite Goring called his mother's home. His mother said he had left five minutes earlier for a Mr Hoyte's place.

Police at the alleged scene of the murder

When he returned the call, at about 8:55 p.m., the witness said he told her his car was down, and she invited him to use a truck and get to Workman's, from where he would use one of the four cars at the Goring home to travel to Christ Church.

A gentleman by the name of Mr Bascombe, who was Marguerite's friend, then drove Marguerite and Mr Lee to Mr Smith's home where they met Hyacinth. During a conversation with Hyacinth Goring at the house, Mr Lee became annoyed on learning that Hyacinth Goring had been at the scene when Victor was shot. Also in the course of that conversation, Hyacinth Goring's sister is reported to have said that "when worthlessness was being shared out, Hyacinth got all".

Hyacinth's fifth stop – the crime scene (again)

After that, with the permission of Sergeant Legall who was still at the house, they all visited the scene.

Sergeant Legall arrived at the scene at about the same time as Inspector Clarke, Sergeant Belle and the police photographer.

At the Enquiry, the three policemen all of whom were at Atlantic Shores soon after 'Pele' was shot, reported conflicting descriptions of the scene. Sergeant Legall said he found the car, G29 with only one door opened, when he reached the scene and said there was a stone on top of a heap of clothes lying on the back seat of the car.

According to him, he drew the stone to the attention of Inspector Byron Clarke who told the Commission the stone he saw was protruding from under the garments.

Earlier at the Enquiry, Sergeant David Callender in his evidence, said all four car doors were opened when he arrived at the scene, and Parris was lying face down on the back seat, with one hand near a stone.

However, photographs of the scene taken by Belle showed that the car doors were closed, there was a stain on the ground near the right front of the car, which was said to be a blood stain, and stains of blood on the back seat of the car. A stone was shown to be near the stain on the ground and the paint work of the roof of the car was shown to have been chipped at one point. Inspector Holder, the police ballistics expert, attributed that chip to a bullet fired from the left of the car to the right.

Previous witnesses had testified to seeing one or two shoes outside the car, but police photographs of the scene showed the two shoes in the rear of the car.

At the scene, Inspector Clarke took a statement from Hyacinth Goring. Then for the first time, she alleged that the unknown gunman had robbed her of $1,100.00.

From the scene, the police went with Hyacinth Goring to the Oistins Police Station where her father Charles Goring was, and where she gave a written statement to Sergeant Callender.

Testimony of Corporal David Callender

She was a friend!

Sergeant David Callender, who was the first investigator at the scene of the crime the night *'Pele'* was killed, said he had accepted everything Hyacinth Goring had first told him, because he had known her very well. According to him, she was a friend and not a stranger. The sergeant admitted knowing Miss Goring, her father, and her uncle, who was an Inspector of police and also revealed that he had visited the home of Sergeant Goring (Hyacinth's father) on occasions.

When asked if he was a good friend of the family by Sir Denis Malone, Callender responded "Yes, I knew them fairly well".

Callender said he was born in St George and worked at District 'B' Police Station under Sergeant Charles Goring, for about two years. He said his enquiries into the Parris murder had not been coloured by his friendship or Miss Goring's family connections in the Force. Despite his affiliation with the family, he did not ask to be recused from the investigations because he felt he could have given of his best in the case.

Sargeant David Callender

Sergeant Callender said he left the Oistins station for Atlantic Shores almost immediately after the first report of the shooting incident had been made at about 8:33 p.m.

Description of how 'Pele' was found

He described the scene as he saw it on reaching there around 8:38 p.m; the car G29, with the four doors opened facing the direction of town; Parris on the back seat, with half his body inside the car, and from the waist down protruding through the back door on the driver's side.

According to Callender, 'Pele's' shoes were outside the car, he was wearing socks and he was naked from the waist up, with two shirts piled up on the car's back seat. Callender also noted that he was conscious. With the help of PC Mason, he removed 'Pele' from the car, while Mr Smith held the lamp to assist the police. Callender noticed that there was a stone in the back seat.

He told the Commission of blood stains outside the car and on the back seat near Parris' body, but said he did not see powder burns on the wound, nor blood on 'Pele's shirts.

According to him, Miss Goring related that a dark man, about five feet seven, with a felt hat pulled down over his eyes and white handkerchief across his nose, had attacked them, shot Parris and ran off with her keys and skirt.

Callender testified at the Malone Commission that Miss Goring was wearing a blue blouse and green towelling shorts when he met her at the murder scene, but said he could not explain why she was not dressed otherwise until later.

He did not ask her whether she had shot Parris, or whether she knew who shot him, when he first saw her at Atlantic Shores on May 16th.

The detective told the Commission that he had taken no notes of his first conversation with Miss Goring and when he left Atlantic Shores for the Queen Elizabeth Hospital with Parris, **Hyacinth Goring and Scofield Smith were left behind alone, at the murder scene.**

Callender also stated that although he was not sure what actually transpired the night Victor Parris was killed, he still did not believe Hyacinth Goring to be a suspect in the murder.

However, he told the murder probe commission that he did not believe Miss Goring was telling the full truth.

"Even today she is a very vital witness," Callender told the Commission then. In later questioning, however, the policeman said "while Miss Goring could be a possible suspect... I don't see her as the prime suspect."

He told the Commission that he had reported the inconsistencies of Miss Goring's statement to Inspector Byron Clarke, who was his immediate senior in the murder investigation, but the Inspector had let her go.

Hyacinth's sixth stop - Sandhurst Apartment Hotel

Callender also explained that Miss Goring was taken to Sandhurst Apartment Hotel, at St Lawrence, Christ Church for the police to record another written statement from her, because they wanted to be near the scene of the crime, and because there were no adequate facilities at the Oistins station.

She was later taken to Oistins police station where she stayed until after 2:00 a.m. on the morning of May 17th, 1978. Her father was also there with her and before she left the station with her father, she was told that Pele had died around 10:44 p.m.

Strange occurrences that happened that night

In his evidence which lasted for nearly three hours, the Commission learnt that Callender, the first policeman on the scene of the shooting, had not sought to secure vital evidence connected with the crime.

It was also learnt that the second statement from Hyacinth Goring was recorded by the police at a south coast hotel, rather than the Oistins or any other police station.

There were no forensic tests of Parris' clothing found in the car, or the spot of blood at the scene. The handbag Hyacinth carried was not dusted for fingerprints, nor was it searched.

The clothing she wore the night of the shooting was not held by the police for forensic tests and subsequently as evidence, and when the police learnt that there had been an attempt to clean the same clothing before investigators arrived at the scene of the crime, Hyacinth had already burnt the garments.

The car belonging to Miss Goring was driven from Atlantic Shores to the Oistins station, although in her first statement on the scene to Callender, Goring had said that her attacker had escaped with her skirt and car keys.

The same car was handed over to Miss Goring about nine days after the shooting while investigations were still in progress.

A gent's handbag found in the car and said to have belonged to Parris, was not listed among exhibits removed from the car, and it was believed that it was handed back to Parris' relatives.

In the Enquiry, it was also revealed that two sets of fingerprints belonging to a person or persons other than Miss Goring or Mr Parris, were found near the lock of the car trunk, and the left front door. Those prints did not match those of any criminal on police files.

Callender also told the Commission that in her statement, Miss Goring said she would be able to identify her attacker if seen again, although he wore a hat pulled down over his eyes, and a handkerchief across his nose. However, no attempt was made to ask her how she was able to identify a masked attacker.

"Atlantic Shores a bad place for lovers"

Sergeant David Callender told the commission of Enquiry on January 28th, 1980 that Atlantic Shores was a bad place for lovers. He reported that there had been several reports of armed attacks before and after *'Pele'* Parris was shot and killed there on May 16th, 1978.

He also said he could not recall how many attacks in that Christ Church lovers' lane had been reported, but there had been an incident as recent as the year before (1979).

He testified that sometimes attackers had approached lovers and demanded money, and there had also been occasions where guns had been fired. However, he admitted it was not common in Barbados for criminals to wear masks, and he could not recall any of the alleged Atlantic Shores attacks where the assailants had worn masks.

Callender said he had believed the story Miss Goring gave him when he met her at Atlantic Shores the night of the crime, but he added that he mistrusted her from the same night when she altered the story she told him in her written account at the Oistins station.

The policeman told counsel for the Parris family, Mr Frederick Smith, that he had reservations about her behaviour.

When questioned about the reason Hyacinth was taken to a hotel and not the police station initially, Callender described Oistins station as "a thoroughfare" with no privacy.

He agreed with Frederick Smith that it was common practice for the police to take witnesses or accused persons to other police stations for statements during the investigations of a crime, but Miss Goring was taken to Sandhurst Hotel, because "we wanted a place reasonably close to the crime. We wanted to put her at ease."

Asked why he thought Miss Goring was telling only part of the story on the night he met her, the policeman said that it was common for women to park out in lovers' lanes with other women's husbands, and vice versa and when they were attacked, to hold back certain information from the police.

The day after the murder

Hyacinth Goring was an employee of the Hastings branch of the Royal Bank of Canada. At 6:00 a.m. the day after the shooting, Hyacinth called her friend Beverly and told her of the shooting incident. She told Beverly that Victor Parris was alive but in the intensive care unit at the Queen Elizabeth Hospital. Hyacinth also called a Mrs Nurse, another employee of the Royal Bank shortly after 6 a.m.

She then went to work and shortly before 8:00 a.m., was relaying her story to a gathering of her fellow employees in the rest room, when a telephone call came through for her. It is alleged to have come from Mrs Olga Asgill who regarded Victor Parris as her son and who knew of the relationship between he and Hyacinth.

When the call was over, Hyacinth burst into tears and became hysterical, announcing to her colleagues that Victor was dead. According to the Commission of Enquiry, this was a peculiar announcement as, according to Inspector Clarke, he had told her before she had left the Oistins Police Station for her home that Victor Parris had died. Her father and her boyfriend, Mr Lee had also been told before leaving the Oistins police station that Victor Parris was dead.

The Enquiry noted that the effect created was that Hyacinth was learning about Parris' death for the first time by that phone call, even though she was told the night before that *'Pele'* had died. The Commissioners believed that it was improbable that when Hyacinth called Beverly and Mrs Nurse, that she did not know that *'Pele'* was dead. This drew them to the conclusion that Hyacinth's actions were no more than well-crafted deception. What was even more interesting was that neither Beverly nor Mrs Nurse were intimate friends of Hyacinth, and were not people in whom she would normally confide. In fact, they were both surprised at the call!

Testimony of Egbert Parris!

This was the screaming headline of the ***Nation*** newspaper of February 6th, 1980 when *Pele's* father, Egbert Parris took the stand at the Enquiry. He denied that a pinkish blood-stained shirt, which was used as an exhibit at the Enquiry, belonged to *'Pele'*.

The elder Parris said he had never seen the shirt before, and it looked nothing like the one Victor was wearing on the morning of May 16th, 1978 when he took his son to work.

The father pointed out that *'Pele'* was wearing a plain brown shirt, to match the dark brown trousers he wore. The shirt tendered in evidence was pin-striped, and carried a 14 ½ inch collar, rather than the 14-inch collar that fitted *'Pele'* Parris.

He also told the Commission that his son was not in the habit of taking additional clothes to change at work before returning home.

The pinstriped shirt was purported to be the shirt found in the back seat of the car involved in the night time shooting at Atlantic Shores, Christ Church.

There were blood stains on the left sleeve, and Parris was indeed shot in the left arm, but there was no bullet hole, and no powder burns to suggest the dead man was wearing the shirt when he was shot.

A gent's clutch bag, the whereabouts of which, according to earlier testimony, was unknown, and believed to have been handed back to Parris' relatives, was also produced at the Enquiry with some items which the father identified as his son's property.

The father recognised a wrist watch and an afro comb, which he had given his son, but told the Commission he had never seen *'Pele'* with a stick of lip gloss, which the police claimed was found in the clutch bag.

Parris also disowned a silver bangle as that of his son, and told the Commissioners the slain man used to wear a bracelet.

The findings of the Commission of Enquiry

According to the Enquiry, almost all of Hyacinth's statements contained several inconsistencies.

One event of importance can be found in the evidence of Mr and Mrs Bowen. On the night of the shooting, the couple was visiting the home of Mr and Mrs Gardiner in Atlantic Shores, which was next door to the home of Angus Edghill. Mr Edghill's house was on a bluff to the north and east of the south point lighthouse and it over-looked the Atlantic Shores coast road.

It was about 8:00 p.m. when Mr Edghill who was in his garden, heard two shots. Within seconds of the last of the two shots, Mr Edghill heard screams, whether of a man or a woman he could not say. The screaming, which lasted for some seconds seemed to him to be continuous but may not have been, as Mr Edghill recalled dashing into his house for a few seconds probably to speak to his wife. While hearing the screams, he saw a figure caught in the headlights of a car travelling from west to east along the Atlantic Shores coast road. The figure was running towards the car and it turned out to be a young woman dressed in a blouse and panty.

While visiting the Gardiners, the Bowens had been listening to stereo recordings. Mr Edghill arrived and told them of the shots he had heard, but they had not heard anything. Mr Edghill left after five minutes and the Bowens remained at the Gardiners' home for about another 20 minutes.

On leaving the Gardiners' home, the Bowens out of curiosity, drove to the cul-de-sac at the eastern end of the Atlantic Shores coast road. They approached it from the west. In or near to the cul-de-sac, they saw **three** cars – Hyacinth Goring's car, G29 (and they noted that all its doors were closed), MC613, which was Mrs Smith's car (the same car Mr Smith admitted to using that night), and a third car which they described as low-backed, unlike a Rover, but like an Austin 1800 or 1100 and powerful.

They made a note of the number of the car but could not recall it at the Enquiry. Standing by G29 were four or five persons and someone dressed in shorts who they thought to be a woman. On their approach, the persons by G29, "scampered" into MC613 and the low-backed powerful car. That car "took off," to use Mr Bowen's expression, and sped northwards up the hill towards Enterprise Road. It was quickly followed by MC613. Mr Bowen followed the two cars. In the lead car he thought there were two persons in the front seat. In MC613, he thought there were three – one being the woman in shorts and another individual he thought might be a woman and who, he thought, might be wearing spectacles.

After passing the turn off to Enterprise Gardens, MC613 suddenly turned left. The lead car continued with Mr Bowen in pursuit. He was travelling at over 50 miles per hour. In the neighbourhood of the home of Mr Gale, Mr Bowen abandoned the chase. He saw the lead car swing right and coming up from behind saw taillights disappearing, but whether to the right or left he was not certain.

A few days after this incident, Mr Bowen passed on the above information, including the number of the low-backed powerful car, to Inspector Winfield Cummins. Inspector Cummins stated that he in turn passed on the information either to Assistant Commissioner of Police Broome or to Inspector Clarke. Inspector Clarke denied any knowledge of the information or even receiving it from Cummins.

The Enquiry noted that what was certain, however, was that Mr Bowen's information reached the police because they were able to contact Angus Edghill. There was, however, no record of that information in the police case file. This came to light for the first time in the course of the hearings by the Commission of Enquiry. Inspector Cummins acknowledged that he had received the information, made a note of it at the time, but he no longer had the note. He also said that he had forgotten the number of the low-backed powerful car.

There was therefore no reference to Mr Bowen on the file, even though the information was allegedly passed on to two senior officers. The Commission of Enquiry believed that this was deliberate to suppress, as opposed to simply forget, the information. **They believed that the identity of the low-backed powerful car and its occupants was to be kept hidden.**

The Enquiry recorded that its principal findings on the above evidence was as follows:

1. What the Bowens witnessed was not the departure from the scene of Sergeant Callender and PC Mason with the injured Victor Parris, but the flight from the scene of Mr Smith, Hyacinth Goring and certain unknown persons.

2. The evidence of the Bowens was deliberately suppressed by Inspector Clarke, Sergeant Callender and PC Mason.

3. The evidence of the hospital staff in the Casualty Ward of the Queen Elizabeth Hospital was deliberately suppressed by Inspector Clarke, Sergeant Callender and PC Mason.

4. The evidence of the nurses on duty who attended to Victor Parris in the Recovery Room of the Queen Elizabeth Hospital was never explored by the police.

5. Inspector Clarke did not enter the Recovery Room as he alleged, nor did he give any instruction to PC Mason to take a dying declaration.

6. Mr Smith did not telephone the police officially before leaving his home to visit the scene with Hyacinth Goring as he alleged; he did so

on his return.

7. Mr Smith must have telephoned some unknown persons – probably certain members of the police – before going to the scene in the first instance, as that would account for those persons being at the scene when the Bowens visited it.

8. Mr Smith alleged that he telephoned the police officially before going to the scene with Hyacinth Goring to make it appear that he did not delay in making official contact with the police. In fact, according to the Commission of Enquiry, he did delay as he had instigated a conspiracy to cover up the identity of the person who shot Victor Parris.

9. When Mr Smith visited the scene with Hyacinth Goring, they were not the only ones there as the occupants of the low-backed powerful car were also present.

10. Mrs Smith was aware of the delay occasioned by her husband and of certain activities which took place at her home such as the rinsing and ironing of the blouse of Hyacinth Goring and the cleaning of her skirt.

11. In furtherance of the conspiracy, Hyacinth Goring in the presence of Mr Smith put on a performance in an attempt to delude Mr Jackman and Mrs Hope into thinking that she was the victim of an attack by an unknown gunman.

12. Such a performance was first enacted by Hyacinth Goring before Mr McComie and Miss Williams when she sought their assistance to take her to the house of Mr Smith to get help.

13. Subsequently, the performance was laid on by Hyacinth Goring for the benefit of the employees of the Hastings Branch of the Royal Bank of Canada.

Of politics and murder?

Pitched into the forum of politics, the publicity given to the death of Victor 'Pele' Parris rapidly made it a matter of public concern. The Commission of Enquiry reported that they had been the recipients of anonymous communications confiding where Victor Parris was shot, by whom he was shot, why he was shot and by what means it had been intended to dispose of his body.

The death of 'Pele' Parris was the subject of speeches from public platforms and of articles in the press. The Enquiry noted that the death of 'Pele' Parris had "affected the body politic of Barbados as an abscess affects the human body."

At the time of the general election of 1976, there existed a close relationship between a Member of Parliament and Victor Parris. That close relationship, had come to an end some months before the death of Victor Parris. Mr Bascombe, who was mentioned earlier as the friend of Marguerite Goring, was elected to the office which Victor Parris had held in the Member of Parliament's political organisation for the constituency he represented.

After the politician's success at the polls in the general election of 1976, Victor Parris had been made the acting headmaster of a school established by said politician. He was paid a salary of $150.00 per month. Victor Parris moved on from this job and secured another job at Welcome Inn, which paid him $800.00 per month. Within a few months of securing the job at Welcome Inn, *'Pele'* was dead.

The Enquiry was told that about six weeks after *'Pele'*'s' death, statements made to Mr Egbert Parris by four persons well known to him, including his friend the late Eric Sealy, the leader of the People's Progressive Movement, was that the politician to whom *'Pele'* was previously affiliated, attempted suicide after killing him. The politician personally denied these stories to Egbert Parris. It appeared that the senior Parris did not take these stories seriously, but reported them to his lawyer, Frederick Smith, Q.C. but did not report them to the police and did not question the politician when he denied them. However, Egbert Parris conveyed to the Commission of Enquiry that *'Pele'* was of the impression that he was being used by the politician.

The Enquiry noted that *'Pele'*'s' father was told by Eric Sealy at a chance meeting at the Grantley Adams International Airport in 1979 that three days before Victor was shot, the prominent politician had enquired if he [Eric Sealy] could find someone for him who would shoot Victor. That statement deeply affected the senior Parris who burst into tears. Mr Parris chided Eric Sealy for his delay in bringing that statement from the prominent politician to his attention. Sealy however later denied saying this to the elder Parris, suggesting that Mr Parris must have misunderstood him as he had not stated for a fact that the politician had spoken to him.

Egbert Parris

The Enquiry noted facts as follows:

- Victor Parris and the prominent politician had at one time been close political associates and members of the same political party.

- Victor Parris and the politician had a falling out and ceased to be close political associates.

- Victor Parris was replaced in the politician's political organisation by Mr Bascombe who was a close friend of Hyacinth Goring's sister.

- Mr Bascombe would, on occasion, borrow the politician's car and had used it to visit the Goring family home at Workman's, St George where Hyacinth and her sister lived.

- The registration number of the politician's car was MF37, and the registration number of Mr McComie's car was MA37. It was Mr McComie who picked up Hyacinth at the scene in his car shortly after *'Pele'* was shot.

- In 1978, Mr Bascombe owned a Rover car and so did the politician.

The Enquiry believed that there was a conspiracy involving both civilians and some members of the police to conceal the identity of the person who shot Victor Parris. They admitted though, that they could not point to any credible evidence which suggested that either the motive for the killing of Victor Parris or the motive which led to the formation of the conspiracy was related to politics.

The Commission of Enquiry also discussed a conversation that took place between Hyacinth Goring, her sister Marguerite, and a friend on one hand, and Police Constables Burke, Reid, Medford and Douglas on the other at a DaCosta's shop on June 28th, 1978 as it pertained to the politician's involvement in the death of Victor Parris.

Marguerite Goring was supposed to have said that the politician fitted the description that Hyacinth had given her of the assailant and that the politician was the first person to go to the hospital after *'Pele'* had been taken there.

Hyacinth was reported to have said that the politician was unknown to her, but if she saw the assailant again, she would be able to recognise him. According to PC Medford, Hyacinth Goring described the man as stocky, broad-cheeked with a band around his mouth and that he wore spectacles – a description, according to the Enquiry, to which the politician bore some resemblance.

Hyacinth also added that she had spoken to a man who said he had seen the car, MF37, (which was the politician's car) in the area on the night in question. When asked by P.C. Medford for the name of the man, he said her reply was "That is for the police to find out."

However, the Commission of Enquiry concluded that there was no credible evidence in their opinion, which pointed to the politician being involved in the death of Victor Parris. They believed that the senior Parris' belief that the politician was involved in *'Pele'*'s death was founded on rumour and malicious insinuations. Further, the Commission reported that there was evidence which supplied the politician with a reasonably sound alibi.

Further, the Enquiry found no evidence to support Marguerite Goring's statement that the politician was the first to visit the hospital after Victor Parris had been taken there. The evidence showed that the politician did not learn of the death of *'Pele'* until the morning of May 17th, 1978.

Inconsistencies in Hyacinth's statements

According to the Commission of Enquiry, there were a lot of inconsistencies in the evidence offered by Hyacinth Goring. In describing the assailant, Hyacinth Goring had said that he was not dark in colour, but clear-skinned, and her sister had said she believed that Inspector Clarke, who was the officer immediately in charge of the investigation, was withholding information because he was a member of one of the political parties in Barbados. The account of the conversation given by PC Medford and PC Reid is supported by PC Burke and to some extent PC Douglas. There is no statement on the police file that records Hyacinth Goring's account of this conversation and she declined to give evidence before the Commission of Enquiry.

The Report of the Enquiry stated that they (the Commission) had no reason they could consider for three police officers to invent the above conversation. They, however, strongly believed that Hyacinth Goring was **"a stranger to the truth and was given to invention and fabrication."**

They reported that her description of the assailant was contradicted by descriptions previously given when she spoke of the man as black, stocky and bearded and made no mention whatever of his wearing glasses. She had also said of the assailant that he wore a hat pulled over his face which, if true, would suggest that she would be in no position to describe the man's face.

However, two policemen, Constables Merlon Reid and David Douglas in their evidence before the Malone Commission, disclosed that Miss Goring told them the assailant at Atlantic Shores had broad cheeks and was wearing glasses the night he shot Parris.

They both told the Commission about being introduced to Hyacinth Goring and her sister, Marguerite and of Marguerite telling them of hearing rumours that a prominent government minister had shot Parris.

Reid told the Enquiry that Marguerite Goring informed him that the description her sister had given fitted the politician.

Miss Goring described the assailant to Reid, as "stocky and wearing glasses, and she said a man had told her of seeing the car MF37 in the Atlantic Shores area the night Parris was shot".

"We asked her for an identity of the man (who saw the car MF37), but she declined and said it was for the police to find out," Constable Reid testified.

There was evidence that seconds after shots were heard, a car was seen leaving the area where Victor Parris was found, but that car had never been traced. They also believed that Inspector Clarke withheld evidence.

The Commission of Enquiry was of the opinion that the conspiracy was conceived to pervert the course of justice by concealing the identity of the person who killed Victor Parris. They reported that a false impression was created that the killing of Victor Parris was of the lover's lane type. That is to say, a killing of the male lover accompanied by robbery or rape, or as alleged in this instance, the attempted rape of the female by an unknown assailant.

The Commission also found Goring's explanation, which she had given to account for her presence in a dark and lonely place at 8:00 p.m., strange. They did not believe that she could have been viewing land at that hour. Then too, the description she had given of "talking" in the car to the man who later was shot, was, according to the Enquiry, explicable only if one supposed that she was too embarrassed to state the obvious conclusion to be drawn from her lack of attire, which was that she and her companion were love-making as she did not at the time suggest that she was without her skirt and was shoeless.

Hyacinth also alleged that the man who shot *'Pele'* and tried to rape her, also robbed her of $1,100.00. She had made no prior mention of money, but only referred to her 'things' when she spoke to Mr McComie and Heather Williams. Hyacinth had told the Smiths that she had offered the gunman money and had left her bag with the money in it in her car when she made her escape. She had previously stated to the Smiths that she had given money to the man **and he had refused it.** She however, later told Inspector Clarke that the man who shot *'Pele'* robbed her of the money.

Hyacinth also told Sergeant Callender that the man had run off with her skirt. But within minutes of her saying that, Mr Smith's evidence was that he saw her take her skirt from the car while Sergeant Callender and PC Mason were removing *'Pele'* from the car. Sergeant Legall also testified that when he arrived at the home of Mr Smith at about 8:50 p.m., Hyacinth Goring was dressed in a skirt which matched her blouse and was the type of skirt that was worn then as a uniform by female employees of the Royal Bank of Canada.

Hyacinth's story about the skirt changed yet again. In a statement taken from her by Inspector Clarke on the afternoon of May 17th, 1978 her explanation for not being dressed in her skirt when picked up by Mr McComie was that at the command of the man who shot *'Pele'*, and with the sanction of *'Pele'*, she unbuttoned her skirt. In running around the car to where *'Pele'* lay after being shot, the skirt which she had forgotten to refasten, dropped off.

Another inconsistency is that Hyacinth told the Smiths that her keys were in the handbag she had left in the car. Yet, according to the Commission, less than half an hour passed when, according to Sergeant Callender, she told him that the man who shot *'Pele'*, had run off with the switch keys of her car. The switch keys were later used that night to enable the car to be driven to the Oistins Police Station. Later, in her evidence to the coroner, she conceded that the man who had run off with the switch keys must have brought them back that night.

Love triangle (or square)?

The story of the switch keys is of interest from two aspects. One is that before the coroner, Hyacinth explained that it had been her intention to get *'Pele'* to the Queen Elizabeth Hospital but because the man had run off with her switch keys, she could not do so.

She said that as a consequence, she tried to get Mr McComie to assist her but he refused to help. Mr McComie did not mention that such a request was made to him and that Miss Williams stated that such a request was not made.

The picnic days before Pele's death

The Commissioners in their report said that what they also found interesting about the switch key story is that a little more than a week before *'Pele's'* death, an incident happened a Sunday night around 8 pm when Hyacinth and other employees of the Hastings branch of the Royal Bank of Canada and *'Pele'* were on their way home in Hyacinth's car from a picnic at the Crane Beach.

They had reached the home of Hyacinth's colleague Beverly when Mr Lee came by in his car. Mr Lee was the steady boyfriend of Hyacinth with whom he had jointly purchased four acres of land with the expectation, as he thought, that it would be the site of their future matrimonial home. He was on good terms with the Goring family, and a regular visitor to their home.

In fact, when Hyacinth's sister Marguerite testified in court, she told the Enquiry that the only man Hyacinth used to leave home to go out with was Mr Lee, and her going out with other men was never discussed in the family circle.

Her sister also went on to say that she had never seen Victor Parris, and that the first time she heard about him was the same day he died. She said the day before, Hyacinth was on the telephone and had summoned a friend by the name of Barbara to talk to someone on the other end. Marguerite said the next day, she asked Barbara who was the person that Hyacinth called her to talk to on the phone, and she replied it was Victor Parris, whom she knew from school days.

'Pele' was also seeing another woman named Edna at the time of his death. Edna admitted at the Enquiry into his death that she had been on intimate terms with *'Pele'* soon after he went into work as a Financial Controller at the Welcome Inn Hotel. Edna also thought that she was in a steady relationship with him. However, even though she admitted that she never considered a permanent relationship with *'Pele'*, she did not think he was jilting her for Hyacinth Goring.

She admitted that they had had lovers' quarrels, but their relationship still stood strong until he died. She also never regarded Miss Goring as more than a friend Parris knew at the bank.

Edna admitted knowing of Parris going on a picnic with Miss Goring, but she could not remember the date. She testified that it could have been a week before Parris' death that he talked about the picnic, and told her about an incident later that day when Miss Goring's boyfriend intercepted them on Lodge Road.

Back to the night of the picnic. Mr Lee, on seeing Hyacinth, stopped his car. He was annoyed because Hyacinth was not at her home at 7:00 p.m. as he had understood she would be, and it was then after 8:00 p.m.

According to the Enquiry report, reaching into Hyacinth's car, he removed the switch keys and drove off with them, leaving her stranded. About half an hour later, he returned and handed the switch keys to Beverly who in turn gave them to Hyacinth.

According to the Commission of Enquiry, the story told by Hyacinth of the removal and return of the switch keys of her car on the night of May 16th, 1978 is "such an exact repeat of this earlier incident, that we have no doubt that the inspiration for that story, if the incident it relates did not happen that night, came from this previous incident". They believed that it was too much to expect that within the space of little more than a week, two incidents involving the removal of switch keys and their return, should happen to the same person by the acts of two different persons.

Edna also said she never met Parris' father although she spoke with him on the telephone, and neither did she meet any of his friends.

Their conversations were mainly about sports and his involvement in politics during the time that they were friends.

A woman who described herself as *'Pele's'* adopted mother, Mrs Olga Adzil, told the Commission of Enquiry that the slain man fussed about his "bank chick"

Hyacinth Goring, and told her that his new love was from St George, that her family had a lot of property and that he had "gone into a lot of money".

She believed that *'Pele'* might have been alive today if he had by-passed the "bank chick" and stuck with "sweet cakes", referencing Edna.

Mrs Adzil also felt that Parris was heading on a danger course, after he told her about an incident involving Miss Goring's boyfriend, shortly before he was killed.

"I told him to see the police about it, and leave out the bank chick... I didn't hear nothing more because he didn't do what I told him," Mrs Adzil said.

Mrs Adzil said she knew Parris since 1974, when he taught at an academy, the same school her two children attended.

She also told of Parris visiting her home at Pinelands, St Michael, with friends which included Hyacinth Goring, whom she met about five weeks before Parris' death.

Mrs Adzil said Miss Goring had dropped Parris to her home, and he had called out to her saying "Miss A, this is my bank chick. She (Miss Goring) laughed and everything was alright," Mrs Adzil recalled.

"He phoned me every day and told me about his bank chick," the witness said.

Mrs Adzil told the Commissioners that Parris confided in her and she had gotten the impression that he loved Miss Goring very much.

"He said she was going to the States in August 1979 and that she would send for him and marry him," Mrs Adzil said.

About four weeks before his death, the witness related that Parris went to a picnic at the Crane beach with Goring. The following day, Monday, he called her (Mrs Adzil), as he usually did around lunch time, and told her he had something to talk about.

He started by saying *"Miss A, I nearly get killed last night,"* as he related how Miss Goring's boyfriend intercepted them, pulled the car he (the boyfriend) was driving in front Miss Goring's car, removed her ignition keys and went on down the road, leaving Hyacinth stranded. Mr Lee was annoyed because Hyacinth was not at her home at 7 p.m. as he had understood she would be, and it was then after 8 p.m.

About half an hour later, he returned the keys and gave them to Hyacinth's friend Beverly, who in turn gave them to Hyacinth. Mr Lee told Miss Goring the same way she wanted the keys, he wanted her, adding "If I don't get you, nobody ain't going to get you," the witness said.

According to Mrs Adzil, Victor knew the boyfriend and had told her that they both attended school together.

Later, Victor told Mrs Adzil that Hyacinth Goring had said there was nothing she could have done about the fellow who intercepted them at Lodge Road because her father had accepted the boy, and there was nothing she (Miss Goring) could do to stop him visiting her home, said Mrs Adzil.

Mr Lee allegedly did not know about the affair between Pele and Hyacinth, which in itself is strange considering that he removed the switch out of her car the night of the picnic. The Enquiry reported that Lee said after the night of the murder "I now see when I can't find her where she go," and "smart people always outsmart themselves".

It was said that he appeared annoyed when he found out that Hyacinth was in the company of another man, and he was not aware of Hyacinth's friendship with 'Pele' after 'Pele's' death. He was told by Marguerite Goring that the man that Hyacinth was with that night that he took away the switch keys after the picnic was Pele.

Was the couple looking for land?

The general belief was the theory that the couple was looking for land in Atlantic Shores that fateful night was flawed. Several persons close to the couple believed that this was *not* the case.

One of the chief persons to disbelieve this theory was Hyacinth's father, Charles Goring. The elder Goring thought his daughter had gone there to make love, according to Sergeant David Callender, when he testified before the Parris murder enquiry.

Callender said he had spoken to Goring at the Oistins police station just after he had completed recording the first statement from Miss Goring.

"I told him his daughter was out with a man... that man was shot and that Hyacinth had mentioned she was up there with a man looking at land."

Callender told the Commission that the elder Goring replied, 'Don't believe her. She was looking for no land. Speaking to you as man to man, she went up there...' "and he used a word," the witness said, "that meant having sex."

'Pele's' self-described adopted mother Mrs Adzil was also one to falsify that theory of looking for land. She described 'Pele' as a spendthrift who had to support his own home and could not have had any money to buy land at Atlantic Shores.

"The only thing that he wanted to buy was a Celica car to take me out driving," Olga Adzil told the Malone Commission.

Mrs Adzil told the Commission that when Hyacinth Goring said she had taken Parris to look at land at Atlantic Shores, her immediate response was "Land! I say, 'Pele' don't want no land'."

Mrs Adzil said that after hearing of 'Pele's shooting, she called Goring at the bank at 8:30 a.m. giving her sufficient time to get into the bank's office at Hastings.

Miss Goring, in answering her questions, explained how she had picked up Parris at Welcome Inn Hotel at his request, and soon after, they had exited the car on reaching Atlantic Shores, the gunman attacked, firing three shots, hitting Parris with two, and later escaping with her car keys.

Asked whether she was sure Parris had not asked Miss Goring to take him to Atlantic Shores to see land, Mrs Adzil replied, "Yes, sir. It came strange to me, and he does tell me everything he does do."

One member of the Commission queried whether *'Pele'* ever mentioned wanting to buy a house. "The only thing that he wanted to buy was a Celica car to take me out driving," Mrs Adzil answered.

When quizzed regarding knowledge about *'Pele's'* financial position, Mrs Adzil also told the Commission "a gentleman like him always spending... I don't think he had money. He had to support his home and he used to give me a little something."

Mrs Adzil remembered that when she asked Hyacinth Goring whether she still planned to travel to the United States, Miss Goring replied, "That [the shooting] can't stop me from going to the States, because I have given my evidence already."

'Pele' shot at point blank range

According to pathologist, Dr Belfield Brathwaite, Victor *'Pele'* Parris was shot at point blank range, with the gunman no further than eight inches away. Dr Brathwaite, who performed the autopsy, told the Commission that the fatal shot was fired from above, at a 45-degree angle, and suggested that the assailant was either much taller than Paris, or that the victim was kneeling when he was hit.

The shot entered the left shoulder, penetrated the left lung and lodged in the spine towards the back in the fifth rib space in that area.

Dr Brathwaite told the Commission that Parris had probably gone into a state of semi-consciousness, and eventual death resulted from shock and haemorrhage, but *'Pele'* could have lived if he had received medical attention within two hours of being shot.

Dr Brathwaite also told of certain other external injuries, including a bruise near the temple and a broken tooth, which seemed pretty recent, and occurring about the same time as the fatal shot. They were consistent with a fist or blunt instrument of some kind.

Brathwaite said it was his opinion that the broken front tooth could have occurred from a blow by a fist, or a stone, or by the deceased falling on a stone.

There was little external bleeding, and the doctor said the blood stain on the roadway was also consistent with a person lying in that spot for some time.

The doctor also explained that Parris would have gone into immediate shock on being hit by the bullet and that there would have been danger of paralysis. The victim would have been so affected, the doctor added, that he would not have been able to use the lower limbs, although it was difficult to determine over what period of time the injury would have crippled him.

Brathwaite added that the external bruises resulted from some sort of violence, explaining that although the blows to the skull were not sufficient to cause uncon-sciousness, Parris could have been in a state of semi consciousness for more than two hours, and in a condition to talk.

The Commissioner's views on the events

The Commission of Enquiry came to the conclusion that the inconsistencies and varying versions of Hyacinth's story suggested to them that when taken together to make out a prima facie case, Hyacinth Goring's story of an attack by an unknown man was false. They believed that she created a false impression either because she herself shot *'Pele'* Parris or she knew who shot him. They believed that either version explains why she was not afraid to return to the car as she knew there was no gunman and rapist there.

They believed that she was in a state of undress not because the unknown gunman had ordered her to remove her skirt, but because while she was having sexual inter-course with *'Pele'*, she shot him or he was shot by someone she knew.

In the end, the Enquiry reached the conclusion that *'Pele'* was killed by Hyacinth. In a section of their 231-page report, which was laid in Parliament in November 1980, said "other features of the evidence fit the finding that it was Hyacinth Goring who shot Victor Parris when he was outside G29 and she inside it. One fact according to them was that despite the fact that it was dark and despite her story of having escaped from the gunman who, according to her, had shot *'Pele'* when he was outside G29 and she inside it, Hyacinth was able to tell Mr McComie and Miss Williams that *'Pele'* had been shot in the arm although the wound was very small.

"We submit she knew he had been shot in the arm, not because she had pulled him into G29, as that was another of her false stories, but because it was she who shot him. So, also, her innumerable falsehoods, including her story of the removal and return of the switch keys, which we now can say was not only false in the reason given for it and in its description of the person who shot Victor Parris, but was false in itself because it was not an account of an incident that happened that night, are explained.

"The motive behind that story, we suggested, was similar to the motive that prompted the description of the assailant given by Hyacinth Goring to the three police constables at DaCosta's shop on June 28th, 1978 and her statement then that she knew a man who had seen the car MF-37 in the area of the locus in quo on the night of May 16th, 1978. It was a subtle attempt to remove suspicion from herself and to throw it upon another."

They also believed that the Smiths initiated a web of conspiracy, of which some members of the Royal Barbados Police Force were interwoven. They believed Mr Smith summoned the conspirators who came in the low-backed powerful car and also because on each occasion that the police went to the cul-de-sac, a call was first made at Mr Smith's house. The Enquiry concluded that there was a cover up and suppression of information among the Smiths, some of the police involved and Hyacinth.

The Commission of Enquiry also believed that Mr Jackman and Mrs Punnett-Hope, who Hyacinth and Mr Smith visited, after leaving the scene, were being used by the latter to support the illusion of an attack by an unknown man, and were mere pawns in the game. The Commissioners asked the important question: Why did Hyacinth disclose that she took a bath and cleaned her blouse? What was the urgency in disclosing that information?

Hyacinth refuses to testify at the Enquiry

When the Commissioners of Enquiry commenced their public session, they were informed that Hyacinth Goring was in New York City. The Commission was going to leave Barbados on January 30th, 1980 for the United States to interview Hyacinth Goring. However, Hyacinth advised in a letter from New York that she had no intention of testifying before the Enquiry either in Barbados or in New York or anywhere for that matter. Essentially, she declined either to return to Barbados at Government's expense to appear before the Enquiry or to give evidence before the Enquiry in New York City. The Commissioners never had the opportunity to meet Miss Goring. According to the report, due to the fact that they never met her or had she replied to criticisms made of her, they did not feel constrained to withhold any comment whether favourable or unfavourable, regarding the statements that were made as she was given the opportunity to appear before the Enquiry.

Could Miss Goring have been brought back to Barbados?

Barbadians were calling for efforts to ensure Miss Goring's return to Barbados at all costs after she bluntly refused to give evidence to the Commission of Enquiry.

Furthermore, there were no extradition laws between the governments of the United States and Barbados that would allow her, even as a key witness, to be brought back to Barbados to appear before the Commission.

Only in the case of an accused person do the extradition laws come into effect. Miss Goring had not been accused and therefore could not be brought back.

When the report was laid in Parliament, then Deputy Prime Minister Bernard St John said no charges would be brought against Goring, and none of the other criminal proceedings recommended by the Commission would be brought. According to him, a letter sent to the Attorney General by the Director of Public Prosecutions said that on the evidence available, no charge of murder would be brought against Goring. "The evidence, he said, was not of the nature, quality and kind which would enable the prosecution to prove all the essential ingredients of those charges to the standard required by the criminal law.

The Commission of Enquiry cost the Barbados taxpayers bds$183,000.00.

Interviewing Goring

Retired detective, Sylvester "Slater" Williams remembers well interviewing Hyacinth Goring.

"She was one of the most difficult witnesses I ever came across in all my policing. She answered like a police and never volunteered any information for a follow-up question. She answered what she was asked and nothing more," Williams said.

He said he found it difficult to interview her, as he used an interrogative technique which was successful in the past, but not with Goring. "From the way she answered questions, she was "tactful" and very careful in answering questions, but he could not say for what purpose. However, he found her cooperative, but possibly concealing information.

"I was puzzled as to why she had to be so careful in her answers," he said. "I tried to find out but I failed."

Williams said he thought Goring was truthful when she said she could identify the man who attacked her and Parris at Atlantic Shores.

Hyacinth returns to Barbados

Ten years after 'Pele's' death, around Christmas 1988, Hyacinth Goring returned to the island briefly staying with her relatives in St George. The **Nation** newspaper sent a team to the house on December 27th to speak with Hyacinth. However, she was not at the house when the team arrived.

When the journalist told the male who was at home at the time to 'Please tell her we will be back," he replied "No, you won't!" The team tried unsuccessfully by telephone to speak with Hyacinth after that.

Prior to this, in December 1980, **Nation** reporter Tim Slinger tracked Goring down in New York where she told him, "It's not the way people think it is. Someday I will return to Barbados and clear my name." That day has not come and 'Pele's' murder remains unsolved.

CRIME SCENE DO NOT CROSS

CHAPTER FIVE

The Gruesome Canefield Murders of the 70s and 80s

Here the cane fields silently loom,
Dark and ominous under the moon,
Its roots, the remnants of scattered tombs,
Flesh and bones, an unfortunate doom.

Something's in the shadows, whisper ghostly cries,
He will bring you here, where you will die,
Cold and alone, your corpse lay bare,
After he traps you within his snare.

Andrew Power, *Night of the Gathering fields*

Few persons born in the 1980s and beyond would know of the era in Barbados when there was a chain of murders referred to as "the cane field murders". It was a scary time for Barbadians. A serial killer was suspected to be committing the heinous crimes, and was believed responsible for the murders of at least five women.

The modus operandi of the murderer was to discard the bodies of these women in cane fields or bushy isolated areas.

According to **Nation** Editor, Carol Martindale, women were put on the alert for months to not venture out at night or after certain hours; to be wary of approaching strangers and to reject offers of rides.

The man suspected by police of raping and murdering these young Barbadian women between 1973 and 1982 is still at large. He is also wanted for the attempted murder of another woman, and was identified by investigators as the person who unsuccessfully tried to rape at least four other females.

There was widespread speculation that the suspect was from the upper echelons of society. Police operated on the lead that the women were duped into attending fake job interviews and there might have been an element of pornography before the victims met their tragic demise.

Like Dash, Robinson's handbag with means of identification was left at the scene. As in Dash's case, a hammer and knife were left. Like Turton, jewellery, a wrist watch and a chain with pendant were left with the body.

In all cases the throats of the victims were cut in a circular motion from the left under the neck and a knife wound was on the arm.

No reasonable attempt was made by the murderer to prevent identification of the victims.

At the time, a number of young women island-wide received calls from an unknown person to keep an appointment at various points for job interviews, with offers to pick up the women.

Sandra Robinson, one of the victims left home in response to a telephone call to keep an appointment for such a job interview.

It was also suggested that Margaret Turton may have gotten a ride to go to a job interview.

These are the cases.

GOLDA DASH

G olda Dash, 18 years of age at the time of her disappearance, lived in Vaucluse Tenantry, St Thomas. On Monday, March 12th, 1973, Golda left the home of her father, Alonza Dash at 6:45 a.m to go to work at Yankee Garments in Grazettes, St Michael and never returned home.

Golda attended Lawrence T. Gay Primary and then went on to Springer School. According to her sister-in-law, Nancy, Golda was a quiet girl who attended the Phillipi Pentecostal Church in Shop Hill, St Thomas, where her cousin was the pastor. She was also the mother of two girls, Judith, two years old and Juliette, nine months.

Golda Dash

In the two weeks that Golda was missing, scores of persons from the neighbouring communities searched for her, day and night without any sighting or clue of her shocking disappearance. According to Nancy, searches extended from Christie Village to Shop Hill "and all over" hoping to find her. The young and old joined the search for Golda. Police were constantly in the area looking for clues and questioning the family about Golda.

The discovery of Dash's body two weeks later signalled the beginning of a chain of mysterious disappearances of females and the grisly discovery of their bodies in canefields.

On March 27th, a dog turned up with a skull at Applewhaite's Plantation, St Thomas. The skull was part of the remains of Golda, which were later found in a canefield at Applewhaites, St Thomas on March 28th, 1973. At the time of her disappearance, she was wearing a knitted multi-coloured top and a brown skirt. She was identified by a Marva, who she had left the baby with while she went to work that day.

Police had no clues as to who would want to harm Golda. Persons who were close to Golda at one point or the other were interviewed, but investigators were unable to establish a link between them and Golda's death. The case grew cold.

Fifty years later, there has been no word on the case of the murder of Golda Dash. The family however, has not forgotten Golda. Juliette Dash was just nine months old when her 18-year-old mother's body was discovered in a cane field. In an interview with the *Nation* newspaper in 2004, Juliette lamented that the only thing of substance she has of her mom Golda is a photograph. She remembers nothing about her mother, no recollection of being nursed by her mom, not the comfort of being cradled, not her face, not her smile, not her words, nothing.

She told the *Nation* that as a result of her mother's untimely death, she and her older sister Judith, who was then two years old, were raised by their uncle and his family.

"It was hard not knowing a mother. I feel I was cheated of a mother," Juliette said at the time. "I was teased a lot at school for not having a mother. I used to cry," she recalled.

Juliette said the murder of her mom impacts her life in how she relates to people, and "I find difficulty trusting people."

However, even though it's been 50 years, Julia would still like closure to the murder of her family, and expressed the desire for the police to find the person who robbed her of her mother's love.

"I always wanted to know what happened. They [her family] said they [the police] picked up various people, but had to let them go because of insufficient evidence.

"I would like the police to try to find out what happened on that day. They should try to put an end to it so I can put an end to it," said Juliette.

One of Dash's older brothers, Ryeburn Phillips of Black Rock, St Michael was only a few years older than she was when he heard about his sister's murder.

"Golda was a quiet person; she wouldn't harm anyone. Her murder was very difficult for me because we were very close and at the time, I was the only one of the brothers here in Barbados.

"I called the rest of the family and they came down shortly after. Our mother was in England at the time; she took it very hard. What made it more difficult was there wasn't a body to be seen, just bones and so on," he said.

While Phillips would like police to find his sister's killer, he is sceptical that police will get any closer to the killer now than they were back in the 70s.

"I would like to get some closure, yes, that is the only thing left now. But... I felt the police didn't work hard enough, but I wish them luck," he said as it related to reopening cold cases, a decision made by then Commissioner of Police Darwin Dottin.

Orene Wilkinson, a resident of Applewhaites, remembered how she felt as a young mother in her 20s when she saw a glimpse of Dash's body being carried away by the coroner.

"When they found the body, I had just had a twin. I heard about it and went to the scene but all I saw were her feet covered in stockings. I remembered a dog carried the bones into Applewhaites plantation and that was how they found out it was somebody's body in the cane field.

"That was something. Upwards to now, I still get scared at night and I don't really go out".

JANET SMITH AND CHERYL MCCOLLIN

Janet Smith

There were two other ladies who were found murdered in similar circumstances in the 1980s, but there is little documented information on their lives or deaths. Nine years after Golda Dash's murder, 35-year-old Janet Smith was found under a bush by a golf caddy at Sandy Lane Golf course in St James on October 18th, 1980.

Janet left her Mount Standfast, St James home for the Queen Elizabeth Hospital where she reportedly arrived safely. She left the QEH around 8:00 pm and tried unsuccessfully to reach her father that night. She was seen at the Transport Board Depot the following morning but was never seen again after September 25th, 1980.

According to media reports, Smith had reportedly had a history of mental illness after an accident and subsequent brain injury. She was the mother of a two-year old son at the time of her death.

Cheryl McCollin

Cheryl McCollin was a 15-year-old girl from Bridge Gap, Goodland, St Michael. A decomposed body was discovered in the cane fields of Belle Plantation, St Michael on April 4th, 1982. The body had two gold capped teeth, one in the shape of a heart and the other in the shape of a zodiac sign, similar to the deceased.

MARGARET TURTON

Margaret Turton was a 23-year-old female who lived between Stadium Road, Bush Hall, St Michael with her boyfriend, and Bank Hall with her brother, Theodore. She was the youngest of eight children. At the time of her disappearance, Margaret was working at Chefette Restaurants, Rockley in Christ Church where she had been employed for approximately ten months. She was also the mother of Mark, who was five years old at the time of her death.

Margaret was reported missing on August 16th, 1981 after she failed to return to her Bush Hall residence. Her sister, Cyralene Toppin said that she usually went home by bus or taxi, depending on the time she left work.

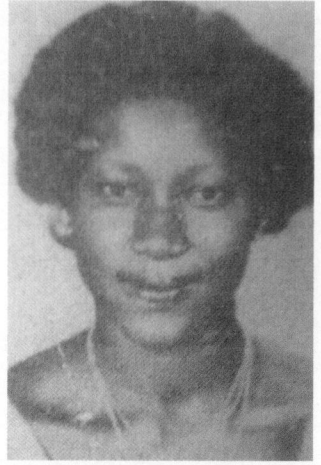

Margaret Turton

Nine months later, a skeleton, believed to be that of Margaret's, was discovered in a burnt canefield at Kent, Christ Church on May 19th, 1982.

Canecutter, Cleophilus Crawford, showing where he saw Margaret Turton's skeleton

Although positive identification could not be given at the time of discovery of the body, it was believed to be that of Margaret.

Police reports indicated at the time that the skeleton found around 10:00 am bore a bangle and a gold chain with the name Margaret inscribed on it.

A medical officer who visited the scene, said the remains indicated that it was a female of the black race, who was in her 20s. He also added that she had been dead for more than three months. Turton was last seen on August 16th, leaving her workplace wearing three gold chains, one of which bore her name.

Remembering Margaret

A memorial service was planned by Turton's relatives for May 30th, 1981 at the St Matthias Church.

Margaret's brother remembered his sister as one who loved a fashion statement. "She loved to dress up," he said. He said she so loved to dress up that she would dress up to go to work and then change into her uniform at work, changing off again to go home. He also remembered her as someone who loved to party. "She was a very cool person, very nice," he said.

Her son Mark said while he was too young to remember much about his mother, he remembered that she was a dark woman who loved to take him on the bus with her. He also remembered that she liked to feed him a coke sweet drink.

After she died, Mark said he was raised by his paternal grandmother and aunts, and they told him how his mother always had him dressed immaculately and well put together.

While Margaret's murder has never been solved, the family believes that the person who robbed them of their loved one is no longer alive. In any event, they believe the person will answer to God and not to man.

SANDRA ROBINSON

Sandra Robinson of Long Bay, St Philip was a young vibrant 23-year-old in the prime of her life with a lot to live for. Someone yet unknown, robbed her of the opportunity of living a long and prosperous life when she was murdered in May, 1982.

Sandra left the home of her mother Melastein Robinson of Long Bay about 11:00 a.m. on May 19th, 1982 in search of employment and was never seen alive since. It was reported that she had left home for a job interview.

Her half decomposed body was found by a police dog on June 5th, 1982 in a cane field at Vaucluse, St Thomas after persons in the cane field who were

Sandra Robinson

participating in a Crop Over Cane Cutting and Piling Contest, found a woman's underclothes and handbag and alerted the police.

According to reports, an identification card bearing the picture of Robinson was found nearby. Police were called in and Inspector Merlyn Watts stated shortly afterwards that it was hardly likely that the owner of the clothing would be found alive.

While police were contemplating pooling manpower from nearby stations to comb the fields, the tracker dog "Ben" arrived on the scene with its handler, and in less than three minutes, one of the detectives shouted to Watts that they had found the body.

Police dog handler and tracker dog on scene of discovery of body

The sergeant said that the body was naked except for stockings, a wrist watch and shoes. Although police did not confirm that an identification card had been found, the arrival of the woman's mother, Melastein on the scene seemed to have indicated that the body was that of Sandra. The scattered clothing included panties, brassiere, petticoat and a blue skirt and blouse. There was also a black handbag that contained a Barbados identification card with the dead woman's name on it. A pair of spectacles was also found.

Reports stated that police found a knife, and that the victim's throat was cut. At the time, Senior Superintendent of Police, Charles Lunn said that there was nothing yet to suggest that the case had any link with the two others whose bodies were also found in a cane field.

He had stated that although the pattern could not be overlooked, there was no direct connecting evidence which was enough to suggest a link.

Shop Hill Tenantry, St Thomas resident Monica Drakes-Byer recalled the fear that gripped her district when Robinson's body was found.

In an interview with the press, Mrs Drakes-Byer said "With the girl Robinson, I had just come from work because I used to work in Westbury Road, St Michael, and when I come up in the bus, I hear they got a woman up in Vaucluse dead and I run up there and when I run up there, the police wouldn't let you see she".

In 2007, a lady in an interview with Ricky Jordan, journalist at the **Nation** newspaper recalled how 25 years prior, she responded to an advertisement in 1982 seeking employment with an agency. She was directed to a house in Maxwell, Christ Church, but a sixth sense warned her about the man's intention and she refused to be led down a dark pathway after an initial interview with the man.

She got away, but she was one of the lucky ones. Golda Dash, Margaret Turton, Sandra Robinson and Cheryl McCollin were not that fortunate. For sure, Sandra Robinson had also pursued a job advertisement which she had circled in a newspaper shortly before she went missing in June 1982.

The lady, who was 53 at the time of the interview said, "If I had gone through that dark passageway, I wouldn't have come back. It is only the Lord's mercy I'm alive today, I'm sure of it."

She had seen a print advertisement requiring sales assistants and, according to her, being young and desperate to be independent, she responded without thinking. "I think the ad was for packaging curry and black pepper. I called the number and a gentleman with a foreign accent gave me directions to get out of the bus opposite a road leading to Maxwell Coast Road. I was then to walk on Maxwell Main Road and count eight houses on the left. "When I got to the eighth house I didn't see any activity so I decided to walk a little farther and I saw a young lady coming out of a house. It was about ten houses after the eighth house. It was an old 'hip house'."

"I will never forget it," she said, pointing to the spot where the now-demolished structure once stood. "As I was going into the house I told the young lady to wait for me. I believe the Lord told me to tell her so because I just didn't like how the place looked," she added. "This man interviewed me and afterwards told me to follow him through a passageway in the house and he would show me how to package the curry and black pepper," she said. But her survival instinct kicked in and she realised that there was no smell of any curry or black pepper. Suspicious, she waited until the man made a move down the passageway, and she headed for the front door. "If he had put me to walk in front of him into the passageway that seemed to lead to a kitchen, I believe I would be gone," she recalled. "Before walking out, I remember seeing about four pairs of women's shoes in the left hand corner of the house.

"I went back out to the young lady and we walked to the bus stop and stayed about five minutes waiting for transportation to get to town. While waiting, we saw a man coming from the bushes opposite the house, bare-backed, and he crossed the road and went into the same house," she said. It was after a visit to the Criminal Investigation Department (CID) that she realised just how close she had been to dying. "They showed us photographs, and both of us picked out a man who the police said was a suspect," she recounted. She said she had since lost contact with the other woman, but believes the suspect was the same man who fled from Barbados after a *Nation* story revealed the police to be closing in on him. "That story had the police catspraddled. The police had a warrant to go to the same house in Maxwell, but the man skipped the island. I understand the man is in his 70s and lives in Miami and the police know who he is," she said. She hoped the police would reopen the case and track down the man not only to bring closure for the several family members and friends of the victims, but to confirm what she had believed all those years: that a split-second decision prevented her from walking into the dark passageway of death. "If the young lady didn't wait I don't know what would have happened to me. If I had gone through that passageway, I wouldn't have come back."

Besides the solid evidence which she believed she provided by identifying a photograph and describing a house in Maxwell, several retired and active police officers who were involved in the investigation made no secret of the fact that they knew who the suspect was and that he had fled some time in 1982, leaving behind the five unsolved murders of Golda Dash, Janet Smith, Cheryl McCollin, Margaret Turton and Sandra Robinson.

(Adapted from the Sunday Sun, January 25ᵗʰ, 2004)

Charles Lunn told the *Nation* newspaper that he had now come back to take over serious crimes and was not involved in the earlier murders. Then came the Sandra Robinson case.

After going over the files on the other cases, he asked the then senior medical officer at the Psychiatric Hospital, Dr Patrick Smith, to put together a team and explain to him these murder cases outstanding.

"We had nothing to go on, and I wanted to approach it from a psychological profile...to see if you could establish a pattern of behaviour of the type of person who would likely commit such a crime.

"Arising out of this team of psychiatrists and psychologists assembled by Dr Smith, they came up with eight names, and among those names [the suspects] was number three in the order they sent them back to me, as the type of persons – with whom they had come into contact in their profession – who would fit into this pattern... of violence and sexual molestation.

"As soon as I got back the report from Dr Smith and this finding, putting together all the other factors and the antecedents of the eight, number three seemed to be the most likely person. We found he was running an office at the head of Reed Street in building and contracting."

Lunn said he ordered a 24-hour surveillance on the man while they pursued other investigations. It was during this time they got the crucial break. A young woman was also attacked in a cane field at Vaucluse, but managed to give her attacker the slip and ran into the plantation's office.

Recalling that incident, Lunn said, "They (the staff) were in the office and about to close when this young woman rushed from the cane field, all panting with her clothes torn, and said she went for a job application, the man told her he had to take her to his partner because he had to discuss it with him, took her into this cane field and pulled out this big, long knife.

"But it was raining that day and in stumbling over some canes, he slipped and she got away from him. So she ran through the canes and he ran behind her, and she told them he was blowing like a cow. She hid in a drain in the cane field.

"After a time, she heard his van drive away, but decided he might be smart, so she remained hidden. From where she was, she could see over some grass and this building, and after a time she heard like a vehicle again passing.

"So she spent over two and a half, nearly three hours from the time she was taken there, based on what we learnt, before she crossed the road into another cane field and ran into Vaucluse office."

Lunn said one of the workers took the girl to Central in Bridgetown instead of District D, where eventually she was interviewed at another police station. The lady was from Ashton Hall in St Peter, and a warrant was prepared to arrest a man for her attempted murder. "It was never executed," said Lunn.

Lunn said though there was not enough evidence to charge the suspect with the Robinson murder, there was enough in respect of the woman from Ashton Hall.

However, when Lunn asked his men to pick up the suspect, he was told the man had skipped the island. He said the policemen tracking the suspect lost him. They watched his wife's house hoping he would go there, but he never showed up.

Lunn said what angered him was that the suspect would have needed a passport and a visa to travel, and he managed to get these and leave the country despite being under surveillance.

He was able to sell his truck and the other equipment belonging to his business, and make arrangements with those he was working for before fleeing the island.

"When I checked, he had a passport three days before I had got on to this girl. He had a visa and they gave him one month. He told the United States Embassy that he was going to visit relatives in Florida."

Lunn said he enlisted the help of the United States authorities here who contacted the Federal Bureau of Investigations (FBI) in Washington.

Through their field offices in Florida, the man was traced to an apartment in Dade County in that state.

"He (the suspect) left the afternoon before the border patrol went to ask for him because they maintained surveillance the whole night and he did not turn up."

Lunn added that "in the course of this investigation, we found two girls from Flint Hall who were attacked. They were given a lift one night by this man, and he tried to run away with them, and they had a big struggle.

"We found a girl off Deacons Road. She also was assaulted by this man and had to fight to get away from him.

"He was renovating a building in Worthing and offered a girl a ride and took her in a cart road. She managed to get out of the car and ran away screaming.

"So when I went to the public with this story, it was to allay the fears. He was a fellow who used to move wild and wrong," said Lunn with a shake of his head. The retired policeman dismissed charges there was a cover-up in the murders to protect politicians, and that some of the deceased girls were seen in blue movies, saying these were just innuendo.

As to how many murders the suspect may have committed, Lunn said, "We don't know. I can address Margaret Turton, Sandra Robinson and Golda Dash."

He said despite there were nine years between the Dash murder and that of Turton and Robinson, "everything about the Golda Dash murder... The modus operandi, from the psychological profiling and the evidence available to me suggests it was the same person who killed all three".

In a separate **Nation** interview with Sylvester *"Slater"* Williams, he said he was haunted by "the one that got away".

"We had a suspect and I believed he was the man, there was too much evidence. I spoke with the Superintendent of the Psychiatric Hospital back then and she had a dossier on him.

Williams recalled that he handpicked then Detective Simon Baptiste who reported during the daily briefings that one morning just when he would have approached the suspect, he [the suspect] had a child with him. Williams gave the order to pick up the suspect the next time regardless. However, there was no next time.

Media spooks the killer

The detectives had a break when they traced a newspaper advertisement that Sandra Robinson responded to in 1982 before her missing report turned to one of murder. Police made a connection with Golda Dash's body recovered in March 28th, 1973.

With the breaking news that police were closing in, the killer fled. Williams revealed that they searched the suspect's wife's home. They had a trap set, but the suspect was already aware that they were on to him. "We searched too early. He was not there, and by then he was spooked and fled the island," said Williams.

It is now almost 40 years since Turton's death. The cases have grown cold. As Lunn said at the time, "Police worked on it for a few months and it is forgotten. The society forgets it and it finishes." Lunn quite correctly queried at the time how long should a case be investigated. He said that an inquest could give a determination or part determination of what actually happened. If during the enquiry, evidence is revealed to identify someone as the murderer, the coroner's enquiry can be stopped at that stage.

The police are adamant they know who the killer is. Sylvester "Slater" Williams remains certain about the killer's identity as that day in 1982 when he told a Press Conference the police knew who the killer was, but did not have the evidence to stop him getting away with murder.

"We knew who he was and I had a Press conference and said we knew who killed Sandra Robinson, but the evidence was not forthcoming. Life is funny in Barbados, it is who you know, and since leaving the Force I heard certain things that make me wonder. In one case it may be that because of the individual, the policeman does not want to do what he should do. Then there are certain people who know certain things but won't say," Williams said.

How the killer slipped detection and arrest

During separate interviews with the **Nation** newspaper, retired senior policemen, Assistant Commissioners of Crime Charles Lunn and Sylvester 'Slater' Williams believed that the suspect was spooked mainly as a result of "an overzealous press report," which sent him into hiding overseas.

Assistant Commissioner Lunn, in his interview with **Nation** newspaper reporter, Sanka Price on January 25th, 2004, disclosed that the suspected serial killer lured most of his victims through advertisements for a job as a secretary/typist in the classified section of the **Nation** newspapers. No telephone number was given in the ads, and on investigation it was discovered that the P.O. Box provided was fictitious.

According to Lunn, the individual, who was originally from St Andrew, operated an office in Bridgetown, and was married. He fled to the United States and was later traced to Dade County in Florida before he vanished. It is unclear whether the man ever returned to Barbados.

There are some questions and observations. First, could the serial killer be back here in Barbados? Did he quietly slip back into Barbados unannounced, unnoticed as police focus shifted from him to other current criminal activity? Have the police been actively searching for this killer? One observation that cannot be ignored. The police dropped the ball, so to speak, on this case. The killer was known. There was the opportunity to capture him, but poor policing allowed him to evade capture. It is mind-boggling that this person of interest was spotted, but allowed to walk away because he was in the company of a child. Couldn't the child be removed from the man and taken to safekeeping while the man was held? Why was there no bulletin for this man's arrest if indeed the police knew who he was? Why was this man being shielded? He was married, so why was there no surveillance of the house or his family? These unanswered questions and observations lead to more questions, which continue to remain unanswered. Meanwhile, the families never forget and continue to seek closure.

CRIME SCENE DO NOT CROSS

CHAPTER SIX

Lovers Lane Murder at the National Stadium

July 1980 was supposed to be an exciting and festive time in the home of Mark Anthony Bryan because his sister was getting married on July 26th. However, that excitement quickly turned to grief and sorrow for the entire family, as somewhere close to midnight on Sunday, July 4th, Mark was murdered.

Mark Anthony Bryan, 27 years of age, was the second of seven children – three daughters and four sons – born to Mr and Mrs Anthony Bryan. At the time of his death, he was employed at DaCosta and Musson's bond on Country Road, St Michael. He was a member of the Bush Hall Cultural Group.

Mark Bryan

Mark and Celeste*, his female companion, had parked in a lovers' lane near the National Stadium's car park when he was shot through the throat in the back seat of the car he was in. The perpetrator, armed with a gun and wearing a wig at the time of the offence, shot Bryan, then dragged Celeste for half a mile into a cane field and sexually assaulted her. She too was shot in the head and left for dead.

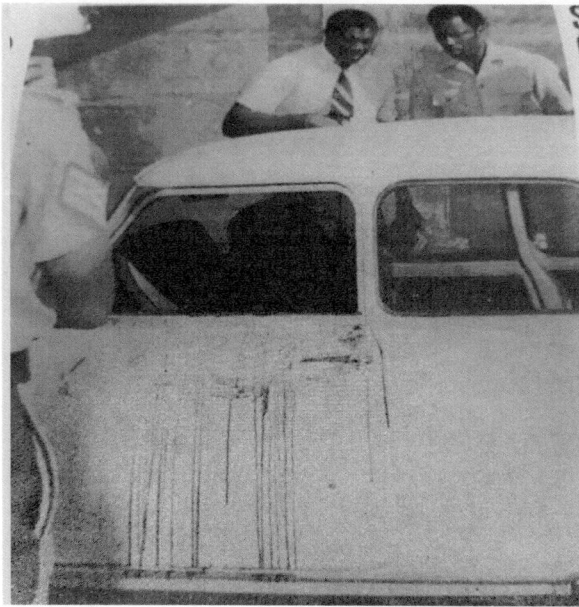

The death car in which Bryan and his companion were parked out

Bryan's body was not discovered until just before 6 a.m. the next day, with bullet wounds under the chin and neck. His wounded companion was later found and transported to the Queen Elizabeth Hospital where she had to undergo emergency surgery to remove a bullet from her head. Fortunately, the bullet had not penetrated her skull and she survived.

Bryan and Celeste were the second couple to be shot within a month in the National Stadium, Waterford area. On June 19th, a St Thomas man was shot by an unknown man around midnight, while his companion, an 18-year-old girl was raped and shot.

Police also revealed that reports came in from the public that someone was throwing rocks in motor cars as they drove through Waterford Bottom.

And so, Celeste was the last link between the police and the gunman who shot them. She was able to tell the police that the killer removed the ignition keys from the car after shooting Bryan, before running off with her.

Police believed at the time they were hunting for a psychopath, so they were forced to actively step up their investigation to ensure there was no repeat of that crime. They later received information that a man living in Bush Hall, whose father had been murdered, could probably be the person who committed the murder, because he was always at home during the day and only came out at night. That person was Errol "*Mopsie*" Farrell.

Errol 'Mopsie' Farrell

Errol '*Mopsie*' Farrell, a labourer of Parade Road, Bush Hall, St Michael was 23 years of age when he came to national attention. The police were keeping surveillance on the Waterford area after reports that the wanted person had stabbed yet another person. On one occasion, he was spotted between the stadium wall and the rifle range and he made a daring escape east of the stadium. He was not identified, but the police had a brief description of a short dark man who could have been the suspect. Farrell did not live far from Anthony Bryan's residence.

Errol 'Mopsie' Farrell

After learning that Farrell was a possible suspect, a squad of about eight policemen, led by Superintendent Arrundell 'Orrie Pomp' Greenidge moved in on the suspect's house - a small single roof house in Bush Hall - about one o'clock one morning. '*Mopsie*' lived with his grandmother at the time. On seeing the police approaching the house, he immediately tried to escape through the back door, but was cornered by the police who were observing at the back of the house. Police had to jump through an open front window to ensure that Farrell was apprehended. After he was captured, he was handcuffed and the police started searching the house. They noticed a piece of cardboard that served as a low hanging ceiling. 'Orrie Pomp' climbed a chair to take a closer look. When he looked on top the cardboard, he saw a hat made from plaited coconut leaves, with a silver gun hidden beneath it. Several masks and wigs were also found at Farrell's home.

The home of Errol 'Mopsie' Farrell

Celeste soon recovered and identified '*Mopsie*' Farrell, and the gun found at his home was identified as the same gun used in the murder of Mark Bryan and the serious bodily harm offence, along with seven other offences.

On the day of his first court appearance, hundreds of people gathered around the courts and the Central Police station to get a glimpse of the accused man. However, they left disappointed as the appearance of '*Mopsie*' Farrell was switched to the Court Prosecutor's office at the Central Police Station. The unusual decision was the result of fear for the accused's safety in the large gathering of the court yard.

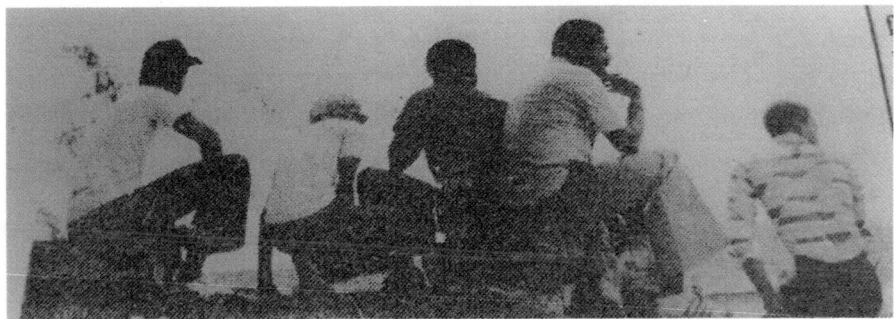

Persons at the court yard waiting to get a glimpse of 'Mopsie' Farrell

The trial

Errol *'Mopsie'* Farrell went on trial in April 1981 for the murder of Mark Bryan and the attempted murder of his companion. In his trial, *'Mopsie'* tried to put in a plea of insanity and his defence counsel called Dr George Mahy of the Psychiatric Hospital, as well as Superintendent of Prisons, Leon Donovan, to support the insanity plea. However, Dr Mahy said he found no positive evidence of psychosis in the accused. Rather, he found Farrell to be alert and pleasant, but it was difficult to assess his intelligence.

A police sergeant told the court under oath that when Farrell, was charged with the murder of Bryan, he remarked, "Murder? ... Oh, Lord!"

Inspector of Police, Arrundell Greenidge, testified that when he visited the house of the accused, he found a gun in the ceiling under a straw hat, along with four rounds of ammunition.

Greenidge added that he also found a pair of dungaree pants under the cellar with what appeared to be blood stains and noted that when he asked the accused to account for the stains, he replied:

"I kill a fowl for my grandmother Sunday; that is the blood from it on my pants."

The Inspector said when Farrell was asked to say something about the gun, he remarked, "I buy that from a man to protect myself."

Companion tells of night boyfriend was killed

At the trial, in the number 4 Assizes, members of the jury were given the details of that fateful night by Celeste, Bryan's companion.

Celeste told the court that she and her boyfriend has just finished making love in the back seat of a car, when a man came up to the window, shot her lover, pulled her out of the car, took her about half a mile into a field of young canes and had sex with her twice.

The woman said in evidence that the attacker had a gun and a torchlight in his hand, that Bryan was about to go into the front of the car, and that she had seen the accused twice before the incident at Eagle Hall.

She added that the accused was wearing a brown shirt, a blue and white knitted woollen hat and that he had bold eyes, and long hair across his forehead and down the back of his neck like a wig.

Celeste said that the accused told her to walk, or else he would kill her, and when they reached the field of young canes, he told her to stop and take off her bra, but when she refused, he produced a knife and cut it off. The witness said that the accused said,

"You ha' money? I man want money!"

With that, the woman said the accused pushed her down on a piece of dungaree pants, took off his pants and underwear, and started to have sex with her.

She stated that after he had finished having sex with her for the second time, and she got up to take up her clothes, she heard an explosion, felt a shot in the back of her head and fell down.

The witness said she could not see anything after that, but she heard what appeared to be the voices of a man and a woman, and the next thing she knew she was at the Queen Elizabeth Hospital.

She said she saw the accused at Central Police Station and under cross examination by defence counsel, Frederick Smith, QC, the witness said she was afraid.

Bryan's sister, Delores also testified at the trial. She told the court that she was at home lying in bed reading a magazine when her brother asked her to borrow the car. The next time she saw him was at the National Stadium lying in the car dead.

Also giving evidence was Shirley Bryan, the father of Anthony. He told the court that the last time he saw his son alive was on July 10th, when 'Tony' was at a shop in Roebuck Street having fun with some of his friends.

He said that as a result of a telephone call, he went to the National Stadium at about 6:30 a.m. on July 14th, 1980 where he saw his son in a car with his pants off in a crouching position.

Errol *'Mopsie'* Farrell pleaded not guilty to the murder of Mark Anthony Bryan. In his defence, Farrell in an unsworn statement from the dock, tried to use the unsolved murder of his father to justify his crime and to plead guilty by way of insanity. He said:

"My father was murdered... I was close to him... I remember going out in July... Something happened, but I don't know what happened."

His lawyer, Frederick Smith QC did not deny that his client shot and killed Bryan and ravished Bryan's partner twice and then shot her, but he argued that he was insane at the time.

Smith argued that the accused's father, Lloyd Lynch, was fatally shot some eight years prior, and that no one was convicted for his death. He pointed out that Farrell had, as a result of this, nursed some feelings of resentment for the system, and had finally erupted violently on the night of the incident.

Using a quote from the Bible, "Judge not that ye be not judged," Smith told the jury that they were in the unfortunate position, as they were the one judging the accused, and urged them to return a verdict of not guilty by reason of insanity.

In his address to the jury, Deputy Director of Public Prosecutions, Elliott Belgrave pointed out that the accused knew what he was doing, and urged the jury to reject the plea of insanity which was put forward by the defence.

Belgrave said that it was clear from the evidence that the accused did not have any disease of the mind, but that he went to the National Stadium with a wig, a glove and armed with a gun and knife to commit a crime.

He added that his actions were not those of an insane person, but that of a cool, calculated customer who had sex on his mind.

The prosecutor said when the accused got to the stadium and was looking for sex, having met a man from the same district whom he would have had to know, and whom he knew would have been able to identify him, he (the accused) shot him to shut him up.

He added that the accused then dragged the female companion far into the field of cane because he did not want to be discovered, and that he shot the woman because he knew that she was the only person who could possibly identify him as the culprit.

The jury agreed with the prosecution, and deliberated for a mere 15 minutes before returning a verdict where they found '*Mopsie*' guilty as charged.

When the clerk of the court asked him if he had anything to say before the judge proceeded to sentence him, he shook his head, looked straight ahead and whispered under his breath "No sir."

Mopsie to go to the gallows

'*Mopsie*' was sentenced to be hanged on April 30th, 1981 for the murder of Mark Bryan between July 13th and 14th, 1980.

Justice Lindsay Worrell proceeded to read his sentence saying "Errol Farrell, you have been convicted of the crime of murder. The sentence of this court is that you be taken from this place to the place whence you came. That you be there kept until the time of your execution, that you there suffer death by hanging and that your body be buried within the precincts of the jail where you last shall have been confined, and may the Lord have mercy on your soul".

With sirens blazing, he was taken to Glendairy Prison, Station Hill to await his date with the executioner.

Mopsie executed

On a dark, gloomy morning on October 10th, 1984, Errol Farrell, along with two other condemned men were hanged at Glendairy Prison. Many Barbadians remember hearing the gallows swing for what seemed to be the last ever that morning, as well as the chorus "*Mopsie*' gone." They were the last persons to be executed at the prison, and in Barbados to date.

* The name of the victim's girlfriend was changed to protect her identity.

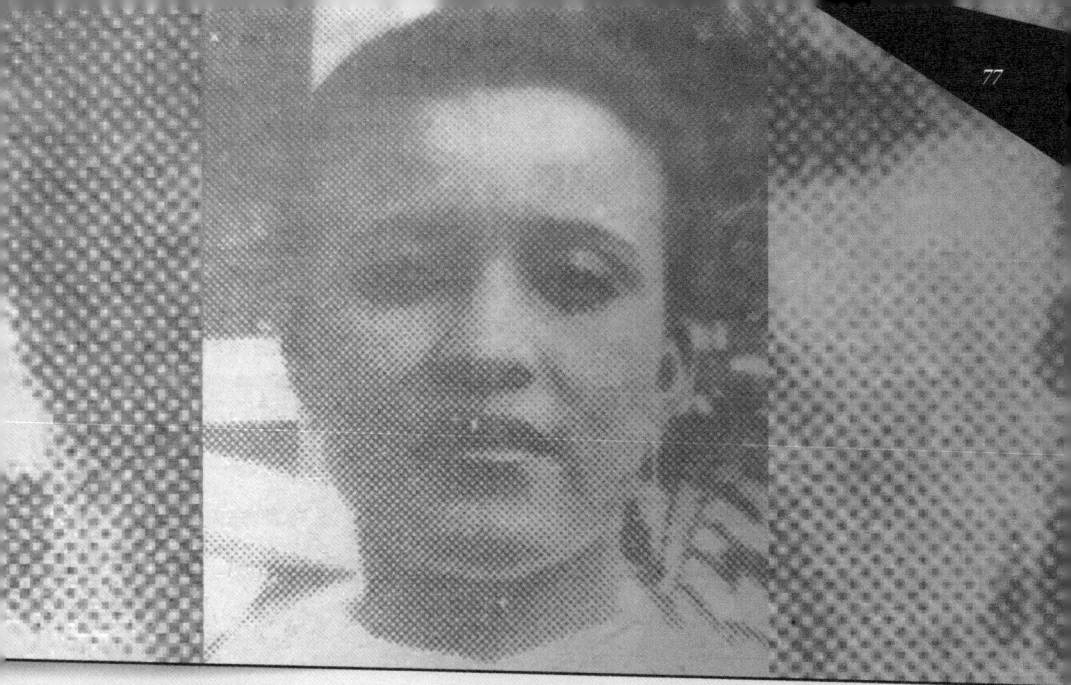

CRIME SCENE DO NOT CROSS

CHAPTER SEVEN

Abduction and Murder on the way to Church

B orn to Isalene and Harold Skeete, Esther, 21 years of age, was one of nine children born to the couple. Everyone in Upper Carlton, St James knew Esther well. After all, she was a friendly, easy going young lady who was deeply involved in her church, Community Bethel Pentecostal Church. She had previously attended the Springer Memorial School and the Samuel Jackman Prescod Polytechnic.

According to **Nation** reporter, Antoinette Connell, church was her passion and on September 22nd, 1984, the night she disappeared, the plan was to go with two friends, one of them Evelyn Hippolyte, to a Seventh Day Adventist church in the neighbouring Garden, St James at 5:50 p.m.

Esther Skeete

Esther lived between the house of her boyfriend's mother at Lower Carlton and her grandmother Millicent Russell's family home. Esther returned home to cook for her mother and grandmother, but declined her grandmother's invitation to stay and eat as she was running late for church and wanted to get there before darkness fell.

According to Connell, Esther was a safety-conscious person and was not a party person, did not accept rides or favours from strangers, and went where she said she was going and was in the habit of telling her family about any experience she had, no matter how small.

At the Seventh Day Adventist Church, Esther's friend realised she had not turned up and was concerned upon returning home and not hearing from Esther. The alarm was instantly raised, followed by a report to the Holetown police station.

Relatives began the arduous task of searching for Esther. Her body was found nearly 14 hours later about 50 yards from the cart road where she was last seen alive in a neighbouring canefield at Westmoreland Plantation

Around 6:30 a.m the next day, Harold Skeete, Esther's father, following the path of footsteps and broken canes leading into the canefield of Westmoreland Plantation in St James, made the startling discovery of his daughter's body. Her throat had been slashed, she had a head wound, and her underclothes were missing, raising suspicion that she might have been raped. A later postmortem confirmed that she was indeed raped.

With each passing day that the murder remained unsolved, the community was equally unsettled.

Then, at a press conference, Senior Superintendent Sylvester Williams admitted the police had a strong hunch as to who the killer was. A lack of evidence, however, prevented them from making an arrest.

Connell noted that in whispers, people "in the know" began to name a particular man as the killer. When the whispers got louder and louder until someone outright labelled a man of the cloth as the killer, the suspect fled the island.

In an interview with the media 12 years later, Harold Skeete recalled that "I had grief lumps. I couldn't swallow." He said that the stress made him lose so much weight that his pants had to be tied with string to stay on, and his crop of black hair turned grey within weeks.

The Skeete family said that back on August 26th, 1986, the police said they knew who killed 21-year-old Esther, but lacked the necessary evidence to arrest the person.

"The police told me the case is not closed, but I have not heard anything more. It is too long so I don't know what could happen now. But I know somebody know something, but they aint telling me nothing," Isalene said.

No one has ever been charged with her murder.

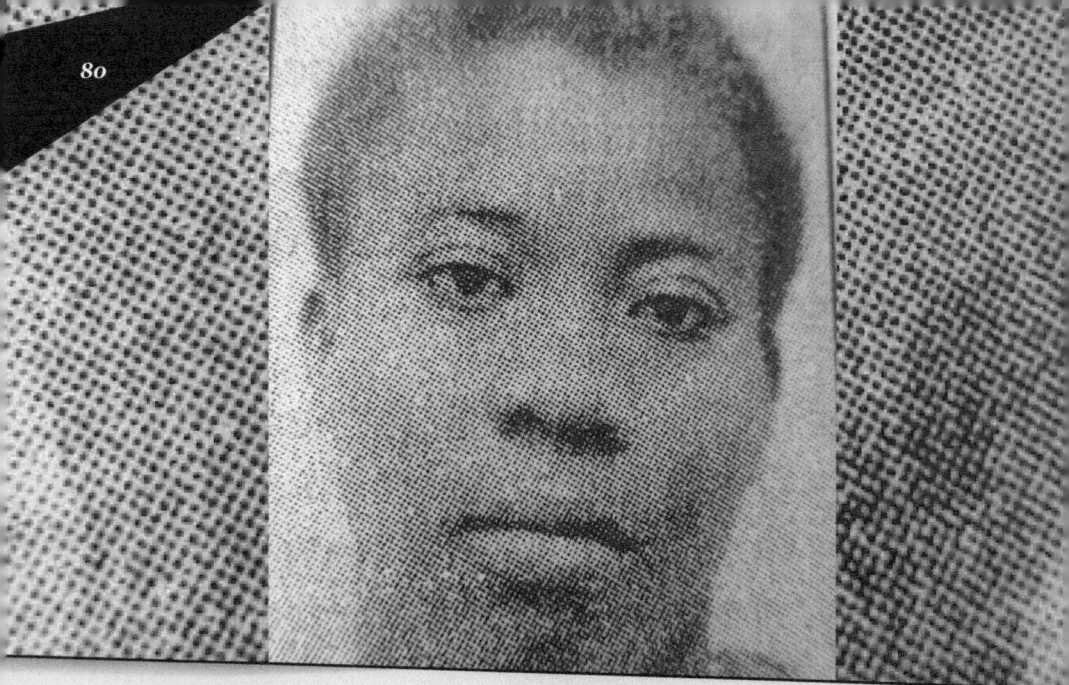

CRIME SCENE DO NOT CROS

CHAPTER EIGHT

A Loved One Never Makes It Home

D oreta Arthur, 34 years of age, disappeared without a trace on Thursday, August 20th, 1987. She left home around 7:30 a.m. to go to work at the Columbian Embassy in Hastings, Christ Church where she was employed as a maid. The last time she was seen alive, she was seen standing, around 8:00 a.m. at the main entrance of the road leading to her home, awaiting public transportation to work. She was described as quiet and obedient and one who would "never dream of sleeping away from home".

Doreta Arthur

Doreta always told her family if she would be home late, and what time she would be returning. Vida Christie, one of her five sisters said the only occasion her sister would not immediately return home after work was when she went to the supermarket. Even then, she would say something" her sister added.

Before leaving home, she instructed her two children, Sean and Antonia to meet her by the bus stop at Shop Hill, St Thomas when she returned.

The children left to meet their mother around 5:00 p.m. and were anticipating their mother's return from work that day. They waited until 11:00 p.m. at that bus stop but she never showed up. When 11 pm came and her sister Vida saw neither the children nor Doreta return, she went to the bus stop. The children were still there and she waited a while longer with them in vain at the bus stop that evening.

A telephone call to the Columbian Embassy revealed that she never arrived there for work that day.

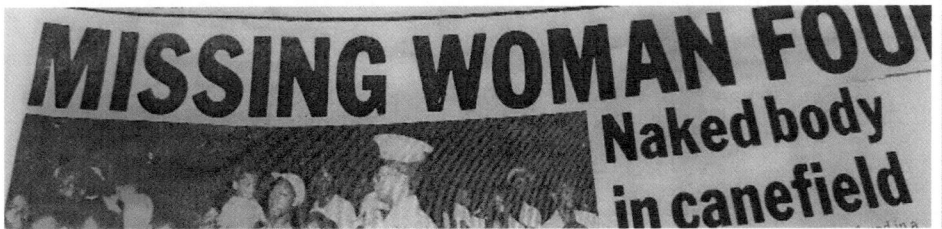

On August 27th, 1987, Doreta Arthur's naked body was located 400 yards away from her Christie Village, St Thomas home where she resided with her elderly mother, Elvira Arthur, her sister Vida and her two children Sean and Antonia.

She was reported missing for one week before a search party of residents, relatives and the police came across her decomposed, headless body in a canefield in the village of Grand View, St Thomas. They had combed the area looking for clues that could lead them to the whereabouts of Doreta. Her body was found 44 feet from the road. Her skull was found about 28 feet from the body and a jawbone was about 6 feet from her body.

The serenity of Christie Village was transformed into one of fear when the news broke of Arthur's disappearance and the discovery of her body. Residents of the area expressed concern about the amount of cane fields in the area. One resident in an interview with the press said that there was also the issue of a lack of street lighting in the neighbourhood. Arthur's death caused residents who travelled the road to Christie Village to exercise even more caution.

Police subsequently arrested and charged a labourer for Doreta's murder. At his trial, Inspector Wingrove Beckles said that he and another policeman went to Grand View Road, St Thomas as directed by the accused, and when they reached a section of that road between two bridges they got out the vehicle and the accused pointed to the northern side of the road and said "I did down behind there when I see de woman coming up the road." According to the police, the then accused directed them further up the road and pointed to an area and said "I hold she bout here so."

Police keeping the crowd at bay

However, in an unsworn statement from the dock, the labourer stated that he knew nothing about the murder, did not know Doreta Arthur, and that he was beaten at the police station by police officers with a hammer and sticks about his body. He said he was taken to River Bay, St Lucy, beaten, a piece of rope tied around his waist and placed over a cliff and pulled back. He told the court at the time that he was told "ya either sign the statement or we going to throw yuh over." He added that the licks got so hot that he decided to sign the statement.

In the end, the jury believed that he was indeed innocent, and a year after her death, a 33-year-old labourer was acquitted of Doreta's murder by Mr Justice John Husbands after a No. 3 Supreme Court jury returned a "not guilty" verdict.

Even though the police are still certain they had the right person, no one has ever been convicted for Doreta's murder.

st YEAR

FRID

ANHUNT ON
OR KILLER

Woman found
dead in field

CRIME SCENE DO NOT CROSS

CROSS

CHAPTER NINE

A Hitchhike
Turns Deadly

B orn on March 7th, 1955, Arlene Marita Watts was a young, ambitious woman who believed she found her calling in the hotel industry. She attended Westbury Primary and St Leonard's Girls schools. After studying at the hotel school, she landed her first job at Sand Acres, and from there she moved to Bajan Rep Services, a tour company, where she was an office manager.

The 31-year-old woman, who was described as a Christian, not just in denomination, but in her approach to people and her work, was found dead in a cane field at Balls Plantation, Christ Church on Thursday, June 5th, 1986.

Hitchhiking a ride turns deadly....

According to police, Arlene Watts and her 20-year-old roommate shared an apartment at Regency Park, Christ Church and were on their way home from a video shop when they were stopped by a man who asked for a lift.

After picking up the man, the two women were "directed under fear" to a cart road at Balls where the sexual assault and murder took place.

According to reports, the other woman, an employee of the Queen Elizabeth Hospital (QEH) managed to escape and reported the attack to Oistins Police Station around 9:20 p.m.

On arrival at the scene, police found the car abandoned in the cart road, but did not discover Watts' body until they resumed their search early on Thursday, June 5th. The body was found about 12 cane rows into the field.

Newspaper headlines on the murder of Watts

Preliminary investigations revealed that Watts died from a slashed throat after she and her companion were raped by a hitch-hiker.

In addition to the slash, according to medical sources, Watts received multiple stab wounds to the body from her assailant.

The male suspect raped the two women and killed Watts around 7:00 p.m. on that fateful night, but her body was not discovered by police until around 8:00 a.m. the next day in a canefield in Balls Plantation, Christ Church.

An intensive search ensued days after the murder, which eventually turned into months especially in the rural parish of St George. Scores of policemen combed the Drax Hall, Ellerton, Greens and surrounding areas hoping to nab the suspect. The suspect was believed to be between 30 and 35 years old.

Police search for the killer

The man, who Commissioner of Police Orville Durant said "we know," was wanted for questioning in Watts' rape and murder. Police were receiving tips from the public, which they found very helpful. Policemen kept watch on the suspect's mother's house and also that of another relative.

However, many people were not satisfied that the police were doing all in their power to capture the suspect. One woman suggested to the media that instead of patrolling the main roads, the police should search the gullies.

The police's handling of the investigation drew the ire of the average Barbadian who believed that the police had dropped the ball in their handling of the case. There was a charge that the police abandoned their search for the suspect after only two hours on the night that Watts was brutally raped and murdered.

Commissioner Durant asked the public to "display a greater level of patience and support for the police... and to give us more of their support" at the stage of the investigations.

He also promised to examine all the circumstances surrounding the investigation and murder. He told the press that if there were any instances of incompetence, he would take steps to ensure the same did not arise in the future.

The funeral

Arlene's funeral was held at St James Methodist Church on June 9th, 1986 to a full congregation of mourners. Hasim Degia, the Director of Bajan Rep Services, where she worked, spoke highly of the young lady who was taken from her friends and loved ones too soon.

In the eulogy, Degia related how Arlene had been one of the top students at the Barbados Hotel School, and started to work as a receptionist in 1973. He also said that she was always willing to accept responsibility, she was a very resourceful worker, and she was not a "clock-watcher."

Police closing in on suspect

On Thursday, June 19th, 1986, police combed Greens, St George looking for the man who killed Arlene Watts.

With a suspect now drawing their attention, they targeted Greens because the suspect had a number of relatives, including his mother, sister and brothers living in the district. It was believed that he had been hiding out in the area.

While the police, with their sniffer dogs searched the area, the small community of Greens was unusually quiet and every window and door of the area remained firmly shut.

The suspect's mother claimed that she had not seen her son for over two weeks and told the police so. She said she had not even had the opportunity to talk to him to ask if he had really done the crime for which he was accused.

Another relative said that she constantly heard footsteps outside her home at night and up to a few days prior, someone knocked on her house as she lay in bed and then a man called out her name three times. She believed the voice was most likely the suspect's, and she spoke to the police about it the next day.

According to her, a policeman who lived in the area, recognised and tried to hold the man near the steps of the Church of God in the district. He was believed to have been hiding out in an uncompleted wall house.

It was unofficially reported that the suspect was hiding under the cellar of a home when a policeman went peeping under the cellar in search of him. The suspect, Lester Harewood allegedly smashed the policeman's face with a rock.

In August of that year, they offered a $2,500 reward for information leading to the arrest and conviction of the man who murdered Arlene.

Lester 'Toffee' Harewood

Lester Leroy *'Toffee'* Harewood turned to a life of crime when he was ten years old. It was in 1958 that Harewood was given four years at the Government Industrial School (Dodds) for stealing.

Seven years later, he began a string of criminal offences, and by the time of his last offence, which was the rape and murder of Watts, they totalled 17 convictions.

He was convicted, reprimanded and discharged for stealing cane in 1965, but it was not until 1973 that Harewood was first sentenced to prison – five years for raping a St Joseph woman.

Soon after his release, Harewood was in trouble again in 1977; this time for assaulting a woman with intent to ravish, robbery, and wounding with intent. He received two five and seven-year sentences, respectively.

Three years later, in 1980, Harewood escaped from prison and while on the run, attacked and wounded a St Michael man who caught him in his home. For that, he was given a five-year sentence, along with nine months, to run consecutively, for escaping from prison.

Caught one year later

Lester Leroy Harewood, 39 years old at the time of the offence and of no fixed place of abode, was charged with the Balls Plantation murder. Harewood, also known as *'Laddie'* and *'Toffee'* stared at Magistrate Charles Harris as 11 other charges were read, including the rape of Watts' companion on June 4th, 1986, and assaulting a St Michael woman with intent to rape her on December 21st, 1986.

Wearing a brown pants, white checkered shirt and white shoes, Harewood, whose hair was unkempt, was told by the Bridgetown magistrate in the packed court room, that he looked "wild and rusty".

Lester 'Toffee' Harewood

Harewood was apprehended on June 2nd, 1987, in a canefield at South Ridge, Christ Church almost a year to the date of the murder of Arlene Watts. A hideout containing a bed, clothing and food was also discovered.

Harewood was slapped with a laundry list of charges. The offences which he was charged with having committed between June 4th, 1986 and May 25th, 1987 were:

Between January 16th and 17th, 1986 – breaking the same bar and theft of articles, valued over $24.00.

- February 2nd, 1986 – breaking Casa Blanca Bar and Restaurant and theft of articles, valued at $6.75.
- May 25th, 1986 – theft of a case of drinks, valued at $24.00.
- June 4th, 1986 – carnal knowledge of a St Michael woman.
- Between June 4th and 5th, 1986 – murder of Arlene Watts.
- September 29th, 1986 – breaking the home of a Christ Church woman and theft of articles, valued at $155.00.
- Between October 24th and 25th, 1986 – theft of a quarter pound of sugar, and two loaves of bread valued at $2.60, property of a Christ Church woman.
- October 29th, 1986 – unlawful and malicious damage to articles, value not exceeding $250.00.
- November 28th, 1986 – unlawful and malicious wounding of Malcolm Evelyn.
- December 20th, 1986 – entering the home of a Christ Church woman with intent to commit larceny.
- December 21st, 1986 – unlawful assault of a St Michael woman with intent to rape.
- December 24th, 1986 – being in the home of a Christ Church woman, with the purpose of committing an offence.

Trial

Police photographer Marson Bayne said he found the fingerprints of Lester *'Toffee'* Harewood on the car in which Arlene Watts and her companion were driving.

He also spoke at the trial of discovering fingerprints on the rear glass of the car's trunk and on the handles of the left and right rear doors.

A police fingerprint expert also said at the trial that he found a positive thumb print of Lester Leroy *'Toffee'* Harewood, on Arlene Watts' car. Sergeant Sidney Brathwaite said on his examination of the car, he found prints of Harewood's right thumb, left forefinger, left middle finger and left ring finger.

Forensic pathologist, Dr K. Sree Ramulu said at the trial that Arlene died as a result of a "cut throat injury" with all the blood vessels, nerves, windpipe and gullet being severed. He went to testify that Miss Watts had ten injuries which had been inflicted before death.

Events of that fateful night

In giving testimony in court, the survivor of that fateful night said Watts and herself, who were friends, shared an apartment at Regency Park, Christ Church and left home in Watts car for Belmont Road, St Michael. About half an hour later, the two friends went to Grantley Adams International Airport, where they made a brief stop before going to the Video Spot video shop in Hastings, Christ Church.

The female companion spoke at the trial of how Harewood, who was standing by the bus stop in front the video shop, asked them for a "ride" to Goddards Supermarket at Rendezvous, Christ Church and they stopped their car to give the hitch-hiker a ride on the night of Wednesday, June 4th.

Harewood on trial

"When he asked for the ride, Arlene told him to get into the car," she said. The woman then relayed that when they reached Goddards, Harewood mentioned that he was going up Rendezvous Hill and said if they were heading in the same direction, he would appreciate a ride there.

According to the witness, they both agreed to give the accused the additional request. The woman said she and her roommate then became involved in a conversation and at one point, actually forgot Harewood was sitting in the back of the car.

"When we turned the hill and were about to go into Regency Park where we lived, it was then I felt a very sharp object like a knife under my neck, the roommate said at the trial.

It was at this point, according to her, that Harewood, in a rough tone, instructed her roommate to keep on driving and told her (the roommate) to get into the back seat of the car with him and keep her head down.

"He told Arlene to keep driving because he had a knife to my throat," said the roommate. The witness also told the court of the tense minutes which followed as Harewood directed the drive along Sergeant's Village and Vauxhall, Christ Church, the Globe Drive-in and Bannantyne until they reached a junction.

The roommate said all along she was held with her head on Harewood's lap with the knife still placed against her throat. As she occasionally glanced from side to side along the route, the roommate said Harewood gave the impression he was living somewhere in St Philip.

She said she lost track of the road after they had reached the junction, and spoke of travelling for about 15 minutes, when she heard Harewood order Watts to turn off the main road. She said the area was a cart road bordered by canes.

The woman said she and her roommate were then both ordered from the car, and Harewood enquired if they had any money.

"The accused asked me if I had any money. I told him I had $15.00. He asked Arlene if she had any money, but she told him she only walked with a cheque book and no cash."

The roommate told the court how the accused man tied up Watts at the back of the car, while he held her at the front for about 15 minutes. She also spoke of how Harewood then tied her feet with a piece of cord and gagged her with a handkerchief before placing her in the car's trunk, which he then closed.

The roommate said during this time, Harewood took Watts from the car away to a cane field. She described her as appearing frightened and unwilling to walk. All this time, Harewood had a knife.

The woman said after the accused and her friend disappeared, she tried to free herself from the trunk, and realised the trunk lid was unlocked. She managed to wriggle out her tied hands from behind her back and later release some string from her feet. By this time, the handkerchief had dropped from her mouth.

She said in an effort not to attract her assailant, she eased open the lid of the trunk and slipped out from the trunk of the car. Describing it as the fastest time she had ever run, she spoke of falling into some mud during her dash to safety, as it had been raining, before she finally reached the main road, where she stopped a taxi driver travelling along the same road.

The roommate said she was taken to the Oistins Police Station by the taximan and minutes later accompanied by the police, she returned to the scene of the incident. She said on her return to the cart road, she saw the car the same place she had left it before her escape. However, there was no sign of her roommate Arlene or Harewood.

The lady spoke of going to the Criminal Investigation Department about a year later, on June 2nd, 1987 where she identified Harewood in an identification parade.

Lester Harewood's statement to the police following his capture at a cane field in South Ridge, Christ Church was read in court as follows:

"I used to go to church with some people in Lodge Road, Christ Church, and I start to get acquainted with some of the members there. One of the brothers from Ashby Land, Christ Church, allow me to live with him.

"One evening in the month of June, 1986, I went down by the Garrison watching a football match. After the match finished, I walk up Hastings

Road, and stop at the bus stop in front the video shop. I see one little boy there. I was going to catch a bus to go back to Ashby Land.

"I see a brown Suzuki car come out from at the Video Spot with two women. I asked them for a lift to Goddards' and the one driving tell me to get in. I get in the back seat. When they get by Rendezvous corner, the women went to stop the car. I asked if she was going up the hill and she said 'Yes,' and I tell she that I was going up the hill.

"When we get to the top of the hill and the woman stop for me to get out, I put my knife to the other woman's throat and tell the woman who was driving to keep driving, because I really wanted some sex.

"She keep driving up the road through Sergeant's Village. I made the woman who I had the knife to she throat get in the back seat, and I hold down she head in my lap. I told the woman to drive straight through Vauxhall. Then after we get right to the top when you pass the drive-in, I tell she to turn left.

"When we get by Balls Plantation, I tell she to swing off the road, and go up through Balls cart road. And when we get 'bout to the half of the cart road, I tell she stop the car and I make them get out. I ask them if they got money, and one say she only got about $15.00. The next one say she don't have any.

"I get some string from my short pants I had on, and I make the young girl tie up the woman who was driving with it. Then I rip off piece of the cloth off my short pants and tie she mouth. Then I tie up the young girl hand behind she back with some wire which I find down by the video place.

"I take away the key from the woman who was driving and make the young girl get out of the trunk. Then I went to have sex with the woman who was driving but she was sick; so I put she back in the car, and take out the young girl out the trunk and had some sex with she.

"When I finish, I tie she back up and put she back inside the trunk. I take back out the woman who was driving again to make she s.... me, but she pull at my balls, and I cut she throat, and drop she in the cane field.

"I decided to kill the young girl too, but when I get back to the car for she, she was gone. I walked back down the road, went through Lodge Road, and went back to Ashby Land. When I get home, my friend was at home; his mother and sisters were at home, but I did not tell anybody anything.

"Then the next morning early, I wash out the clothes I was wearing the night before because I realised that my pants had some blood on it, and I hang them on the line in the yard. The next evening, I hear in Oistins that the police know who the man is that cut the girl throat, so I get frighten and move out from Ashby Land.

"I start to sleep in a boat down Bay Street, and I pelt way the knife in the sea out there. I decide that I did not want the police to catch me, so I stay away from them."

At the trial, however, like most murder accused, Harewood denied any involvement in the cane field killing of Arlene Watts on June 4th, 1986. He said under oath "I was at Ashby Land when the incident took place.... I never leave Ashby Land that day at all, neither did I leave the night." He also denied making a confession to the police, and said he only signed the statement which was admitted into evidence because he considered his life was in danger. He told the Court that the police took him in one of their vehicles to Central Police Station. He said that he was in the back seat with two policemen with his head on one policeman's lap and his feet on the other's lap, and was handcuffed behind his back.

According to Harewood, he was chained to a table and a chair at Central Police Station. He denied making any oral or written statement at the police station, but had signed his name several places because he was threatened. "I never gave the police a statement. I signed due to the fact of certain threats made to me," he had said at his trial.

However, Director of Public Prosecutions, Cecil Tulloch, QC in his address to the jury said that the Crown had produced evidence that identified Harewood as the man who forced the deceased and her companion to the Balls cane field; established the accused's fingerprint was on Watts' car, and produced a statement which police witnesses said Harewood made after his capture.

Urging the jury to return a guilty verdict, the prosecutor told them to pay particular attention to the eyewitness' evidence. Pointing to Harewood in the dock, he asked "Do you think she would ever forget that face?"

Sentenced to death

Lester Harewood was reported to have turned pale when Justice Elliott Belgrave sentenced him to hang on April 26th, 1988, for the murder of Arlene Watts.

Dressed for his final appearance in a dark-blue jacket, matching waist coat, light blue shirt, dark tie and grey trousers, it was reported

Lester Harewood

that Harewood breathed heavily and twitched his fingers as the jury re-entered the courtroom to give their verdict in the five-day murder trial.

In a hushed courtroom, Harewood then 39, received the death sentence after the 12-member jury which included one woman, deliberated for 40 minutes before returning the guilty verdict.

When asked by the judge if he had anything to say before the sentence was passed, Harewood, his voice cracking, replied with a barely audible "no sir".

Lester Harewood had his death sentence commuted to life imprisonment. The 73-year-old Harewood died in prison in October 2022 after spending over 35 years incarcerated at Her Majesty's Prison, Dodds, for the murder of Arlene Watts.

Remembering Arlene

Arlene's best friend from St Leonard's Girl's School, Marilyn Rice-Bowen remembers Arlene as a very cautious and caring woman.

They attended St Leonard's School and sat side by side from first form. She said Arlene was one who never wanted to get into trouble and recalled that she would offer Arlene sugar cakes, tamarind balls or anything else to snack on, but Arlene would always refuse because she did not want to get into any trouble. "She would not take that chance. She was not a risk taker," said Marilyn.

Marilyn had nothing but kind words to speak of Arlene. "She never spoke ill of anyone. She was a very kind, very compassionate person. Any characteristic that speaks positive to a personality is Arlene." They talked about everything and shared everything, and it was only natural that Arlene would be the godmother of Marilyn's daughter Damara.

She also recalled an incident where Arlene saw a man looking through her glass door, and she telephoned Marilyn crying and fearful. Marilyn said she called the police and called Arlene back and stayed on the phone with her until the police arrived at Arlene's home. Such was the nature of their relationship.

That is why Marilyn was very surprised when she heard that Arlene had a room-mate. "She told me everything", Marilyn said, "but she never mentioned that she had a roommate."

"We spoke often, and yet I never knew she was living with someone. I later learnt that she was helping a family member of an ex-boyfriend of hers. This was the type of person that Arlene was – always willing to help someone."

Marilyn recalled the last time she saw Arlene. "It was two days before she died. We passed each other on the road in the vicinity of Maxwell. Arlene said 'I coming by you this weekend'. I told her 'no, not this weekend because I will be at Sam Lord's Castle attending a workshop'. I told her that when I came back down from the Castle, I would call her and we could arrange it for the following weekend, but that was not to be."

"The night that Arlene was killed, the participants of the workshop were all in a coach and passed the area which I now know was Balls Plantation. I saw the car lights out by Balls and we made a comment about people parking out. Little did I know at the time that my friend Arlene was in danger."

"I proceeded with my presentation and only after the presentation was complete, did I hear someone mention that an Arlene Watts was murdered the night before. I went weak. I knew of no one else with that name, and I started crying. I was just crying uncontrollably."

Marilyn did not take Arlene's death well. "Arlene and I were very close; I would walk around and cry, shower and cry, drive and cry. I am surprised I did not go mad," said Marilyn.

Marilyn closed by saying that she will never forget her best friend and wanted to reiterate that Arlene was one of the sweetest persons she had ever met and it was horrible that she had to die the way she did, but she left with an excellent personality that should be emulated by others.

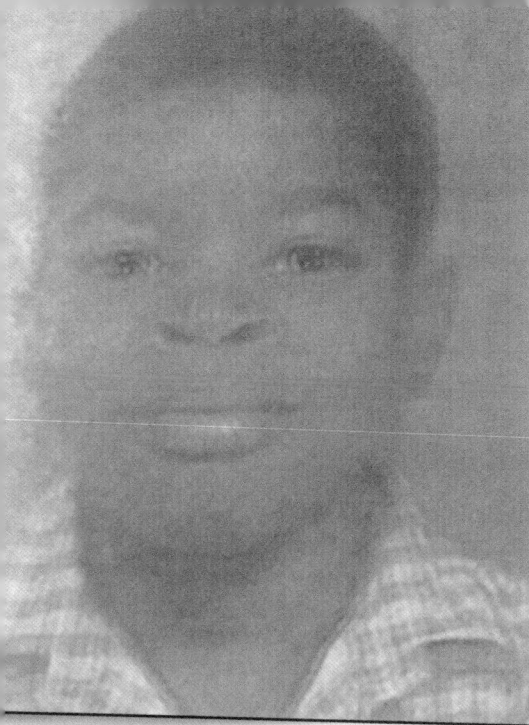

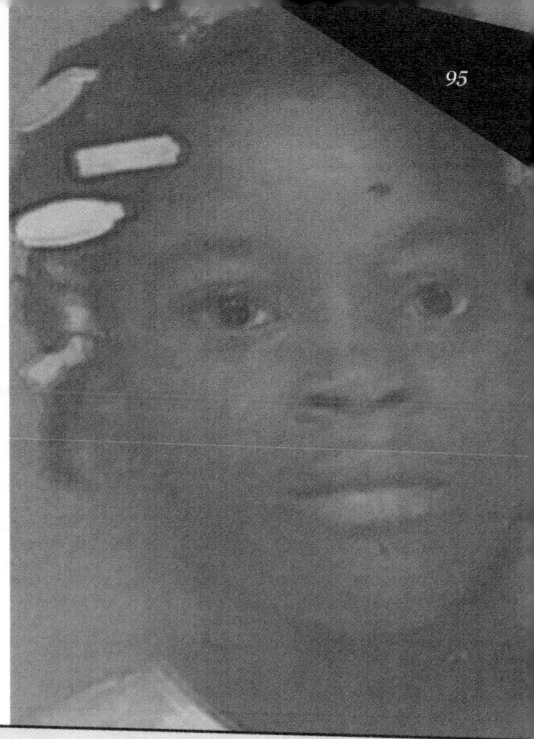

CRIME SCENE DO NOT CROSS

CHAPTER TEN
Daddy Dearest, Daddy Deadliest

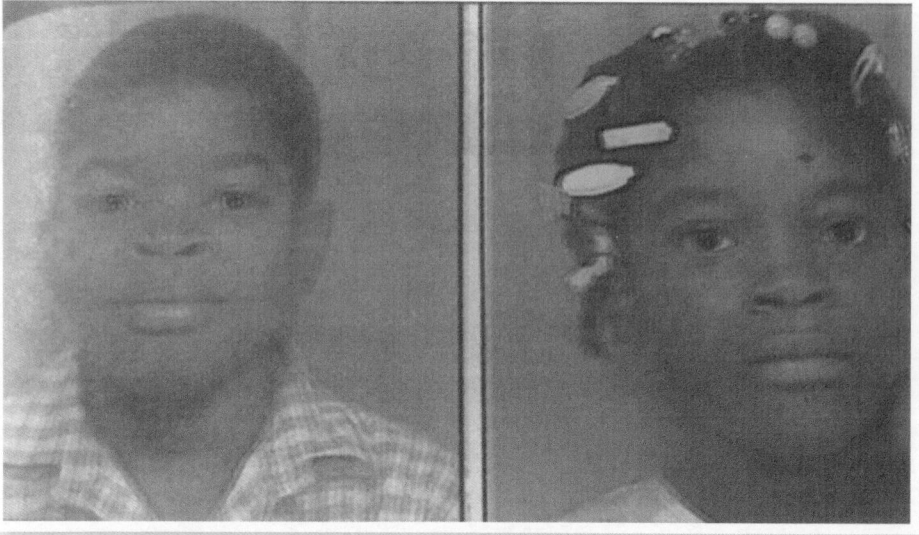

Antonio and Kimberley Gilkes

In the summer of 1992, 11-year-old Antonio and 10-year-old Kimberley Gilkes were to be spending the summer vacation with their father Wayne 'Scarface' Devonish, 30 years old, of Shop Hill, St Thomas. However, by the end of the summer vacation, the lives of the Gilkes and Devonish family would never be the same.

Antonio was about to start his first year in Parkinson Secondary school, while Kimberley was entering her last year in primary school and about to sit the 11 Plus examination.

The Devonish/Gilkes history was one fraught from the beginning with turmoil, conflict and frustration. The relationship between the two families began when Phyllis, the mother of the two children, was forced to move in with Wayne Devonish after she became pregnant with Antonio. Wayne initially wanted to move to his mother's home with his new family, but due to lack of space at her home, relocated a short distance away to Vaucluse Tenantry.

However, Phyllis had health challenges in the form of epileptic seizures, which regretfully took her life when the children were infants. According to Wayne's mother, the day that Phyllis died, Wayne had left home early that morning to go to watch car racing with some friends, and Phyllis was seen later that morning outside with the children. She was later found unresponsive in her bed with Kimberley sitting next to her. Wayne was still at car racing.

Recounting the history of events, Miss Devonish stated that Phyllis' mother returned to Barbados from the United States to bury her daughter. However, unknown to the Devonish family, she had left instructions that Kimberley and

Antonio were to be cared for by her sister and daughter. Miss Devonish said that Wayne believed that he was tricked by the children's maternal grandmother and this led to a breakdown in the relationship between the two families. Wayne was adamant that he wanted his children with him, but the maternal grandmother had already made arrangements with her sister Hetty. Wayne's mother said that she wanted to keep the children, resulting in the matter going before the law courts. However, the outcome of this court matter remains unclear.

Miss Devonish referred to the two children as "two sweet little children" whom she loved dearly. She fondly recalled carrying items for them while they lived in Long Gap in Spooner's Hill. She also said that she would catch the bus which passed where they lived and sit on the left side so she could see them, and shout for and wave at them while she passed by. Such was the love of a grandmother.

Meantime, the relationship between Wayne and the children's caretaker became volatile. According to Miss Devonish, Wayne and Hetty physically fought twice over the issue of the children. However, after this, she would then let him see the children.

As the children got older, they would spend the weekends with the Devonish family, specifically the paternal grandmother, in Shop Hill, where Wayne would come to see them. They also spent the summer vacations with the Devonish family.

However, according to Miss Devonish, Wayne started using drugs and following bad company, who he would link up with and smoke drugs. She spoke harshly with him about this habit, telling him that she did not raise him in that way, and he should desist from these bad habits. However, her pleas fell on deaf ears. She strongly believed that it was the use of these drugs which "triggered him off," coupled with the fact that Wayne and Hetty 'couldn't gree" which pushed him to the edge.

That fateful summer, on July 14th, Kimberly was taken from her home by her father on a bicycle. One week later, on July 21st, Devonish went to collect Antonio. Both children were reportedly seen with their father as they left their home at Sergeant's Land, Fairfield, Black Rock, St Michael. In fact, July 14th was the last time that Kimberly was last seen alive. She was wearing, according to journalist Heather Lynn Evanson, an old dress and slippers, and was supposed to be spending the summer vacation with her father. Antonio was on his way to graduation on July 21st when his father came for him. According to Evanson, his aunt's words were "Your father already got your sister. Don't let him get you."

Initially, the family allowed time to pass hoping that the two children would return in time for school. But hope turned to despair as school started and the children did not return home. After waiting and waiting, the family decided to go public about the children's disappearance.

In the meantime, Miss Devonish said that she took $200.00 to Hetty to give to the children, but she was told that the children were not there and were still in the custody of Wayne. When Miss Devonish asked her son where the children were, he responded that they were with a friend of his.

Two months later, on Wednesday, September 16th, the **Nation** newspaper's reporter Antoinette Connell carried a newspaper article which reported that Antonio and Kimberley were missing for ten weeks. Their aunt, Veronica Gilkes, stated the children were taken by their father from their home. "If anyone sees these two children who are to call me auntie, let me know..." she said.

At this time, Devonish, who occasionally worked odd jobs, and who lived in Shop Hill, St Thomas, was vehemently denying that he had removed the children from their Fairfield, St Michael home. However, family members of Antonio and Kimberly, who became suspicious, informed the press that they had threatened Devonish with police intervention when the children were four and five years old respectively, after he took them from their home and refused to send them back. According to them, the two eventually returned with cuts and bruises inflicted by their father.

On Thursday, September 17th, residents of Shop Hill, St Thomas, where the father lived, were also concerned that the children had not been seen in the area. Wayne had also been missing and the police were trying to locate him. His sister and mother went looking for Wayne and the children asking both acquaintances and strangers if they had seen either of them.

One Sunday, Wayne called his mother, saying he was calling her from a phone booth. When she queried where the children were, he again said that they were at a friend. She started questioning him about this friend, but he said that the children were safe. "All this time, I didn't know that the children were dead," said Miss Devonish.

The children's aunt, Veronica and great aunt Hetty Herbert, their guardians, in a tearful plea, begged that the children be returned safely. Despite a nagging feeling that something was wrong, they kept a vigil which took them to police stations and to Shop Hill several times.

Kimberley and Antonio Gilkes appeared for the first time on the missing person's list on the morning of Tuesday, September 22nd, 1992. Their father, Wayne 'Bonza' Devonish was held by police on the night they appeared on the missing list – September 22nd, 1992. It was around 4:40 pm, when police, acting on a tip off, were called to a bushy area in Shop Hill, St Thomas and cornered Devonish cooking in the Applegrove Gully close to his home. Not far away, police sniffer dogs soon uncovered one of the bodies, the grisly remains of a small skeleton, apparently headless, in a shallow grave. That body, suspected to be Kimberley's, was found in a pit in the yard of her father's home at Shop Hill, St Thomas while the other body, that of Antonio, was dug up about a mile away in Bagatelle from a gully after police were led to it by their father.

One headless corpse with a tell-tale slipper was dug up from a pit in Devonish's yard. What was left of Kimberley's skeleton was taken away in a plastic bag.

The bones of Antonio and Kimberly Gilkes

"I felt it in my heart. I knew those children were dead, even from the day they were taken," Veronica wailed upon hearing the news of the discovery.

Veronica Gilkes, being comforted by a friend

Persons in the community confirmed that Devonish had dug a shallow grave and was cooking using burning wood on top of one of the children's remains.

DEVILISH

'risly end to two missing children

While the police were able to make out that the bones belonged to children, they could not determine how long the bodies had been buried.

However, according to medical practitioners, both children were believed to have been dead for at least a month.

A handcuffed but smiling Devonish was returned to the scenes of the crimes on Wednesday, September 23rd. He was present in the yard where police and officials sifted through the soil in an effort to piece together the remains of Kimberley.

At the roadside where Antonio's more intact skeleton was found, Devonish was confronted by Veronica Gilkes, the aunt of the two dead children.

"Why me, Wayne, I never do you anything?" Veronica said softly.

"I know, I know," was the frank reply from Devonish as he was escorted to the gully.

A crowd from the village where Devonish lived all his life loudly expressed their outrage at the senseless murders of the two children, while Devonish stayed mostly quiet under heavy police guard.

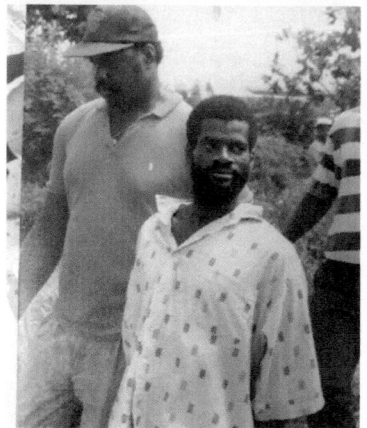

Wayne Devonish

One resident was reported to have said, "These things make you wonder if there's a heaven."

Another elderly resident, after Antonio's body was discovered, said to Devonish "You disgrace your family, you ain't know? You real wicked!"

Devonish responded "Yea, I know."

Devonish, who was described as a loner, looked calm and unperturbed, and even smirked as he acknowledged remark after remark from the residents watching, without flinching.

Kimberley, 10 and Antonio, 11 were apparently strangled and buried, but forensic pathologists were unable to determine how the children died since the bodies were too badly decomposed. Kimberley's bones were worse since they were in an advanced stage of decomposition, and many of them were missing. They surmised that Antonio had been dead one to three months before his skeleton was discovered.

Devonish first appeared in court on the morning of Wednesday, September 23rd, 1992, charged with wounding his uncle.

Meanwhile at Lawrence T. Gay Primary School, children who were classmates of Kimberley Gilkes stood for a minute's silence as a mark of respect for one of their own who was brutally killed. She had been absent from her class 4 since the start of the school term which had commenced three weeks prior.

Antonio had graduated from the school in July, and should have started his secondary education at Parkinson School that term.

Kimberley's place in Class 4 was being kept in the hope that the mystery of her disappearance ten weeks prior would have ended with her being reunited with classmates preparing to take their 11 plus examination.

"I always expected her to return," said her teacher Princess Forde. "I even told some of the students to bring up a desk for Kimberley when they were doing their beginning-of-term sorting out."

"I heard the news about 5 p.m. yesterday (Tuesday), and I was in a sad mood from them on. I cried for much of the night and I couldn't eat anything today," Forde continued.

"Kimberley was usually a very lively little girl; very helpful and the type who would volunteer for anything, so you could always tell when something was bothering her because she would be very quiet."

Did Devonish kill a third child, Glenroy?

According to police and newspaper reports, a third child linked to Wayne Devonish was believed dead. Glenroy Wickham was the only child of his mother, Rhonda. At some point, Devonish was the boyfriend of Rhonda. Witnesses had said that they had seen Devonish walking away with the boy, Glenroy who was six years old at the time. Police had also said that they did not hold out any hope for the missing child.

Glenroy Wickham of 20 Grazettes Housing Area, St Michael, went missing between April and December 1988. Patricia Wickham, his aunt, said that Glenroy was taken away from their Conaught Path, St Michael home on April 10th after Wayne came and took him away on the promise of giving him ice cream, and she was waiting on word from the police on the matter.

Members of the Wickham family said that the last time they saw Glenroy, he was outside their home playing with other children, but when they checked for him later, he was nowhere to be found.

Others said that they last saw him walking in the direction of the Grazettes Community Centre hard courts with a "family friend," namely Devonish. However, Devonish denied knowing where Glenroy was. The police had questioned him, but he denied knowing anything. According to his aunt, the family "searched the whole of Barbados for Glenroy."

Glenroy Wickham

On June 25th, 2010, in an interview with the ***Nation*** newspaper, Glenroy's aunt Veronica Wickham-Bryan, said she still thinks of her nephew "all the time" and "what has happened to him, up to this God-given day." She told the ***Nation*** that the incident "really shook" her family.

"I was not home when it happened; I was at work. Glenroy was outside running 'bout with his two cousins. They [two cousins] said that the fella Wayne called him and he went. They said that he [Wayne] told him that he going and buy something for him. The children said that he [Wayne] was walking. "He [Glenroy] was always frighten for Wayne, but that day he went to him . . . and that was the last time he was seen by any of our family members," said Wickham-Bryan.

She said neighbours, police officers and family members searched many days and nights for her nephew. She said: "We never heard from him and we never saw him. And now, after all of these years, we wonder what happened to him. All of us went searching, then we called the police. The next day, everybody was searching. We went all about looking for him and we couldn't find him and we couldn't find Wayne either. Well now, we give up because we feel he gone. The same guy Wayne end up killing his two children. We said that if he did to his kids that, he did something to Glenroy. He did this to his kids after Glenroy went missing," she said. Reminiscing about her nephew, Wickham-Bryan remembered Glenroy as a young lad who was "active, always running 'bout playing, loved to laugh, read and sing, and he was a bit interfering in your things."

When asked about her opinion on Wayne Devonish today, she said "the day he died, Barbados was one of the happiest places."

Is there a link to Devonish and the disappearance of Thelia Snagg?

Thelia Snagg was a seven-year-old girl who was abducted on her way from school and disappeared without a trace on December 6th, 1988. Twenty-five years after her disappearance, unconfirmed reports indicate that Devonish was connected and responsible in some way for her disappearance as he was known to the family. In a newspaper article dated September 7th, 2014, journalist Timothy Slinger revealed that there had long been a suspected connection between the abduction of Thelia and Wayne Devonish that was never officially made public by the investigators,

A source with knowledge of the case which remains unsolved told the **Sunday Sun** that police fingered Devonish way back in the early 1990s but could not unearth enough pieces to the puzzle to paint a complete picture.

Devonish the person as remembered by those in the community

Many persons in the community expressed shock that '*Bonza*,' as they knew him would commit such a heinous act. They knew him as a relatively peaceful person. However, some persons on reflection said that they were tell-tale signs. One of the biggest signs was that he tried to kill himself when he was younger. They recalled that he tried to hang himself on a tree, but the cord was too long, and an uncle came and cut him down.

Ironically, Devonish almost killed the same uncle years later in a dispute where he beat him viciously with a tennis racket. The uncle was hospitalised in serious condition but miraculously survived, albeit with many head scars which he bore until he died of an unrelated matter years later.

Did the system fail these families?

The family had said at the time of Glenroy's disappearance that they had given the police all the information they had about the child, but the police had persisted in questioning them about his disappearance.

They claimed that the lawmen did not seem to take seriously what some neighbours had to say about the child's disappearance.

Blame Game?

After Kimberley and Antonio's deaths, many questions were asked about their killings. One such question was whether enough was done by authorities to investigate the case of the missing children.

Inspector Glen Gale of the Royal Barbados Police Force's Press and Public Relations Office said at the time "it is not fair to say that the police did not act (to find the children). Throughout the whole exercise, action was taken."

Julius Gittens, journalist at the *Nation* newspaper, reported in the September 24th, 1992 newspaper that the police provided a timeline of their investigations. Inspector Gale outlined that their investigations began two months after July 15th, when relatives said Kimberley left the Black Rock home of her aunt, Hetty.

On September 15th, a call to District "D" Station in St Thomas from Child Care Board officer Roosevelt Gay gave lawmen the first details on the missing children. Later that evening, District "A" Station in St Michael also received a call which was passed on to District "D."

On that same day, officers from District "D" went into action on the matter, according to Gale. "They went into Shop Hill in search of a man called Wayne Devonish. The check revealed that the house (where he lived) was abandoned." Gale added that neighbours told the officers Devonish had not been seen in the area.

On September 17th, two constables returned to "Shop Hill and other areas" in St Thomas. Gale then outlined that on September 18th, Black Rock police joined the investigations. They interviewed Hetty Herbert at her Fairfield, Black Rock home. According to the senior police officer, these follow up enquiries by the Black Rock policemen extended into the District "D" (St Thomas) area, and were largely responsible for the "success" in finding the children's bodies.

When asked if the relatives had not called the police at all before September 15th, Inspector Gale replied "apparently they did not."

But the children's aunt, Veronica Gilkes, who first called national attention to the missing children, told a different story.

She said her first report to the police at Black Rock was on July 17th, just two days after Kimberly left home with their father. About three weeks later, in early August, Veronica's aunt Hetty Herbert, went personally to the Child Care Board with her concerns for the child's safety.

Veronica Gilkes told of being referred back and forth between the two authorities and of repeated calls to the Board and the police. Two months later, on September 15, a few weeks after Antonio disappeared, she said she went to District "A" Police station, after telling her story to *Nation* newspaper reporter Antoinette Connell.

Gilkes explained that it was there that she was told: "Go to the Child Care Board," and then we tell them (the Board) say go to them (police)."

But Inspector Gale, who claimed that he himself called Veronica Gilkes and began to push the investigation, said that he was baffled as to "why the relatives took so long" before calling the police.

He said that a statement is taken from the relative and a missing persons form is filled out. This information is given to Operations Control, the communications hub of the force, at Central Police Station, and circulated to all police stations.

After police have exhausted all their enquiries with relatives, friends and neighbours, and "depending on the circumstances," the Inspector said photographs of the missing person are obtained and distributed to the media.

Devonish was sentenced to Her Majesty's Pleasure in the secure wing of the Psychiatric Hospital after he pleaded guilty to the unlawful killing of Antonio by way of diminished responsibility at the 1993 October assizes.

He later hanged himself from a rafter in the secure wing of the Psychiatric Hospital shortly before 3 o'clock one Sunday morning in August, 2010.

"Something seemed to have upset him during the previous day, something involving a female patient or a nurse," a hospital source said of the former Shop Hill, St Thomas resident.

However, his family is adamant that foul play was involved. They believed that Wayne was in good spirits the last time they say him, but "he kept complaining about this nurse." They questioned how Wayne could have hanged himself with a bed sheet, but yet according to them, no sheets were allowed in his cell. However, the authorities found no suspicion in his death, and it was ruled as a suicide.

That closed a chapter with many unanswered questions. Why did he kill Kimberly and Antonio? What did he do with Glenroy Wickham? Is he really responsible for the disappearance of Thelia Snagg? The answers to these questions unfortunately were taken with Wayne Devonish to his grave and we will never know.

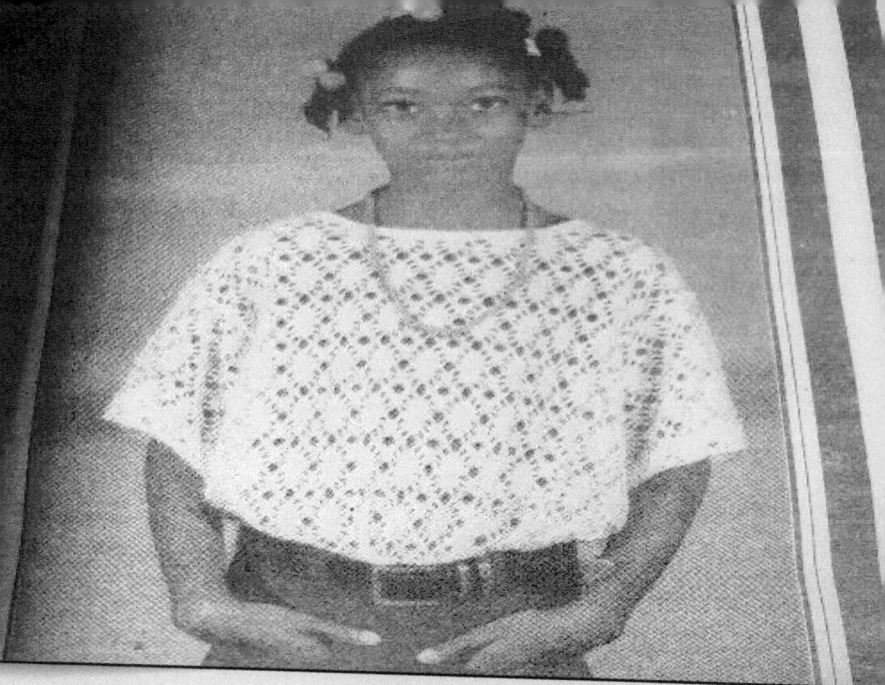

CRIME SCENE DO NOT CROS

CHAPTER ELEVEN

The Gruesome Murder of Little Amanda Newton

O n the morning of Wednesday, July 13th, 1994, Amanda Newton, a pupil of Water Street Girls' School, left the home of her grandmother Inez Newton at Lodge Road, Christ Church to take a package of seasoning to Newton's mother, and Amanda's great-grandmother, Iris Jones, who also lived at Lodge Road, Christ Church.

Amanda went happily along to her great grandmother dressed in a yellow t-shirt, pink skirt and slippers. The little girl usually used a back road to get to her great grandmother's house, which would take her between houses and across the nearby golf course in the Durant's area also in Christ Church and by all accounts, arrived there safely.

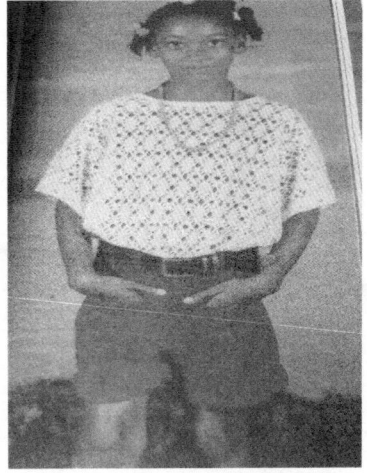

Amanda Newton

The grandmother telephoned her mother's house just after 9:00 a.m. and received confirmation from her niece that Amanda had arrived. Inez's mother, 81-year-old Iris Jones, arrived at her house around 1:00 p.m. and saw Amanda there. She gave Amanda biscuits and cheese to eat. Amanda then went next door to play with her ten-year-old friend.

Expecting her granddaughter to be back home after 1:00 p.m., Inez became concerned when that time came and went and she did not see Amanda. Around 5:00 p.m., she called her mother Iris' house and spoke to her niece who informed her that Amanda had left "ever since". Inez went searching for Amanda without any luck in finding her. She went to different people in the district, asking if they had seen Amanda. By 9:00 p.m., and with no trace of Amanda, she called the police and told them that her granddaughter was missing. The police came to the house and took a statement from Inez.

The next day, Inez went searching again for her granddaughter. With still no sign of Amanda, she was informed that Amanda left her great grandmother's house an hour after arrival in the company of a 16-year-old boy from the neighbourhood.

Her mother Stephanie Jones said she learnt that the boy also went missing on Wednesday and was found early Thursday morning hiding in a chicken coop in his mother's back yard.

Amanda's mother, Stephanie Jones lay in the gallery of her home on July 14th, 1994, her body convulsing as she sobbed, her family and friends gathered around.

On the Friday, two days after Amanda went missing, Amanda's grandmother was told by a landscaper and maintenance man working on a house nearby that he saw a boy about 15 or 16 years old going across the golf course with a little brown skinned girl, about ten years old and pointed out a well to her, telling her that the little girl was in a well at Durant's Golf Course. However, Inez went to the well and looked into it, but could not see anything.

Body found in a well at Durants

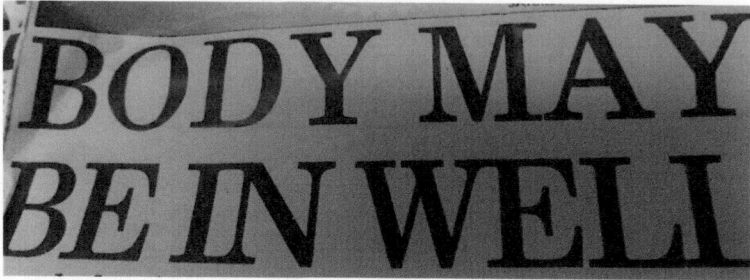

Hundreds of anxious people, many of whom searched for Amanda for the three days she was missing, gathered at the golf course on the Friday, when news broke that Amanda may indeed be in the well, forcing police to cordon off the area.

One attempt was made by a fire officer harnessed to a rope to go into the well, but to no avail; he could only get to 100 feet. Several police officers were seen peering into the well with binoculars and spotlights, but reported that they were unable to tell if Amanda's body was in the well.

Amanda's mother, 24-year-old Stephanie Jones had to be taken to the Queen Elizabeth Hospital after she collapsed several times.

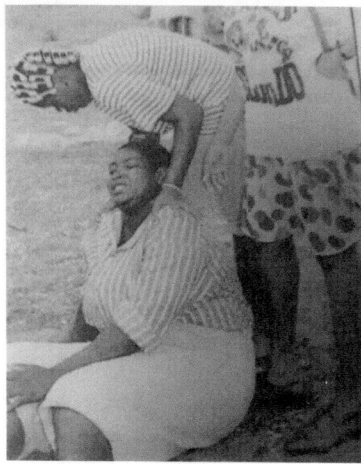

Stephanie Jones being comforted

Amanda's grandmother, Inez Jones, who raised her, indicated at the time that each second that passed was one of agony and anxiety, saying she did not believe that her grandchild was alive.

Police and fire officials spent several hours on Friday concentrating on one of six wells in the area, but were forced to abandon their operation around 8:00 p.m. because of poor lighting and lack of equipment. The well, which also contained about 12 feet of water, was located in the same area where a construction worker at a nearby house was alleged to have spotted Amanda with a rastaman around 3:00 p.m. when she went missing. The man and a 16-year-old boy, who was also seen with Amanda minutes before she left her great-grandmother's house, were in police custody after being picked up at Durants Friday, July 15th.

They resumed the search at 5 o'clock the Saturday morning.

Amanda's mother, who was sedated, kept vigil at the well all morning as more than 30 men from the Royal Barbados Police Force, the Barbados Fire Service, Barbados Defence Force and the Coast Guard struggled to recover the body. This well had also been the meeting point since the day before, for persons who made efforts to get to the bottom of the well.

The **Nation** newspaper broke the story on Saturday that the body of eight-year-old Amanda was believed to be at the bottom of a 140-foot well at the old Durants Golf Course in Christ Church. On Saturday July 16th, 1994, the lifeless body of Amanda, naked from the waist down, was pulled from the well at the abandoned Durants Golf Club. Her mother's anguished screams could be distinctly heard at the same time. The entire community was in shock, and gasps and loud cries could be heard coming from the large crowd of persons who gathered at the scene. It seemed like the Newton family's world came crashing down that moment.

The next day, Inez took on the arduous and heartbreaking task of going to the mortuary to identify her granddaughter's body to the forensic pathologist, Dr K. Sree Ramulu.

A 16-year-old boy was questioned and later charged by the police for grievous bodily harm, which was later upgraded to murder.

Amanda was later buried on Saturday, July 23rd at the Christ Church cemetery.

The preliminary hearing – the case of the controversial leaflet

On August 25th, 1994 at the murder enquiry at Magistrate Court, the prosecutor Station Sergeant Barry Carrington asked the Magistrate for an adjournment. According to the **Nation** newspaper, defence attorney Latchman Kissoon gave his reason for the request for an adjournment. The case began in the middle of the election period, and Kissoon, arguing that the case was prejudicial from the beginning, produced a copy of a leaflet headlined **People's Protest Against Crime and**

Violence. Kissoon noted that the document was being widely circulated around the island, inviting the public to the Garrison Savannah on Sunday, August 21st to "hear the Amanda Newton story first hand."

Kissoon questioned who had the first hand story of Amanda Newton and "if the protestors have the facts about the case, they should supply them to the police rather than try the youngster in public." He then asked the court to make a ruling about the document and "guard this young accused".

However, Magistrate Emmerson Graham said he could not comment on something he knew nothing about, saying that the defence attorney showed him a document, with no knowledge of what happened at the Garrison. The accused was then further remanded.

The trial

The murder trial opened on May 8th, 1994 in the No. 4 Assizes. Throughout the trial, the defence argued on the admissibility of the written confession allegedly given to the police by the accused. The perpetrator contended that he was presented with a statement and promised that if he signed it, he could go home. He claimed that he signed it, but did not know what was contained in it. In the statement, the perpetrator admitted to the police that he drowned eight-year-old Amanda Newton and threw her body in a well after she told him that she was going to tell her mother that he interfered with her.

Then Sergeant Desmond Sands said in court that he recorded a statement from the perpetrator on July 16th, 1994. The statement was as follows:

"On Wednesday, I did out by Archie's picking ackees. Amanda was out there. I went out by the trees by the golf course and Amanda follow me. I tell she I want sex and she said yes and we went out where they does fight dogs [and we did the act] then Amanda jump up and say she gine tell.

"I tell Amanda that she can't tell nobody and she say mek she. I hold she hands and tell she don't tell nobody and she keep on saying I gine tell. Amanda started to pull away but I won't let she go and she scratch me in my face.

"I pull she cross by the burnt out hut and she keep on saying she gine tell on me and I see a can of water in the hut and I put she head in it to frighten she. I had she head in the water for a little while and Amanda went still.

"I started calling she name but she wouldn't answer and when I let she go, she fell to the ground. I get frighten. I thought she did dead and I didn't know what to do so I lift she up and put she in the well side of the hut. She slippers fall off and I throw them in the well too."

The perpetrator said that after he threw her in the well, he went and played football with some friends before going home.

This statement led to a voir dire (trial within a trial) to determine the admissibility of the statements allegedly made by the accused. Kissoon's objection to the statements were that they were not made by the accused; that he signed his name to a written statement which was presented to him by Sergeant Desmond Sands, who was alone, on the promise that he would be released once he signed it; and because of his tender age, he was not informed of his right to have a lawyer or his mother present.

However, Sands testified that he interviewed the perpetrator in the presence of Police Constable Peter Jackson and he asked the perpetrator about Amanda's death and he replied, "she tell me she was going to tell and I pushed her head in some water and she stopped moving."

Sands said he asked the accused if he wanted his mother present, and the perpetrator replied "I can't tell my mother nothing cause she and my stepfather will kill me."

Sands then asked the accused if he wanted to give a written statement and he replied "Yes, cause I did want to tell somebody what happened cause I ain't went to kill Amanda."

Jackson corroborated Sands' testimony.

In court, the perpetrator was shown the confession statements but he said he could not remember if he put his initials on them. He admitted that it looked like his handwriting but he could not remember.

On the first day, it was revealed that the perpetrator disclosed to a doctor that he was scratched under his eyes, but he did not tell the doctor by whom.

Dr Lance Bannister said he examined the then 16-year-old on July 16th, and found two healed abrasions, one under each of his eyes. He told the doctor that he got them from a scratch.

In addition, forensic scientist Cheryl Priddee (now Corbin) told the court that her examination of the clothing and biological samples presented to her produced nothing to link the accused to the murder of the deceased. She did however, find some semen on the seat of the accused's underwear. The forensic scientist received the clothing and samples from Sergeant Desmond Sands who received the clothing from the accused after asking him for the clothes he wore at the time of the crime.

Amanda was alive when she was thrown in the well!

Dr K. Sree Ramulu, the government's forensic pathologist, revealed that Amanda was thrown into the 140-foot well alive.

She died as a result of head injuries sustained in the fall and possibly could have survived for some time after plunging down the well. He revealed that she sustained six injuries, all of which were ante-mortem (before death). Her injuries included a fracture of the left rib; fracture of collar bone, fractured skull, which was broken in five pieces; separation of the skull and laceration of her left lung. He stressed that she did not meet her death through drowning. Explaining her injuries medically, he stated that they showed that she was alive when she sustained the fractures to her head. However, he added that Amanda would have lived sometime after sustaining the injury, but he could not say how long she would have survived without treatment.

Mother: My son is decent

In court, the perpetrator's mother said her son was a decent, obedient well behaved child, who she never had to chastise. She repeated what her son had said to the court and to his lawyer – that he told her he was told to sign the statement and he could go home. He told her that he did not know what was on the statement and they did not let him read it. The mother also told the court that she asked her son if he told the police that he choked the girl and left her under a bush, and he said that he never told that to the police.

Guilty!

On May 10th, 1995, after the three-day trial, the then 17-year-old was found guilty of murdering Amanda by throwing her down a 140 foot well. In an interview before the verdict, his mother said "I already know what the verdict is going to be. The news media and everybody has condemned my child; but I know that whether it is a day from now, or a year from now, they will find the person who threw the little girl down that well.

"I know my child is innocent and whoever throw that little girl down the well, will be caught one day." She vowed to use every channel there was to appeal her son's case.

However, because of his age, he was not sentenced to be hanged, but detained at Glendairy Prison until her Majesty's Pleasure was known. At the time, Justice Elliott Belgrave told the young man that "you will be detained at Her Majesty's Prison until her Majesty's pleasure is known and I hope she takes a long time to express that pleasure".

As he passed his mother sitting in court, she leaned over the bench and shouted "Go long, the Lord ain't sleeping!"

In the courtyard, Amanda's mother Stephanie collapsed on the ground crying hysterically and exclaiming loudly that her daughter was dead. However, Deputy Director of Public Prosecutions, Charles Leacock said to her "Madam, your daughter will rest in peace now. Don't cry, your daughter will rest now."

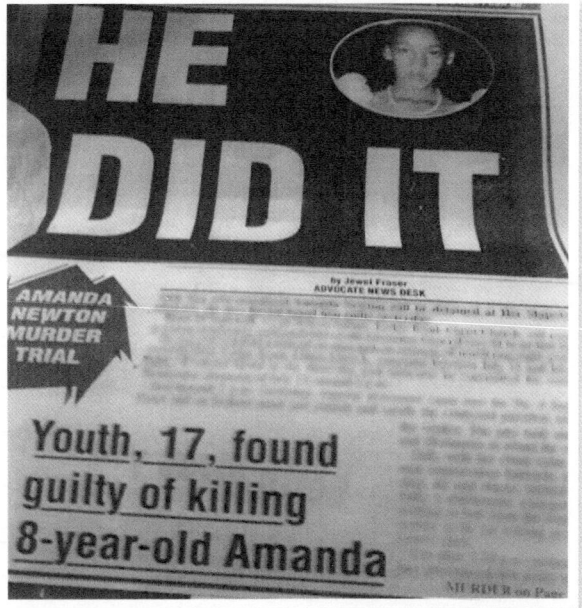

Amanda's grandmother, however, smiled broadly and said "I feel good. I feel good. Thank God justice has been done." She told reporter Gayle Alleyne of the **Nation** newspaper "my stomach feels settled right now. He take my little grandchild and throw her in a well and he get what he deserve.

"It's a sad feeling because I know Amanda can never come back. She is gone with the Lord. Amanda is gone but she's not forgotten. I will always remember she. As long as I got life in me, I will remember Amanda," she said to reporters.

However, the perpetrator successfully appealed his sentence which was reduced to 15 years. After spending 12 years behind bars, he was released in 2006 and reintegrated into society.

Meanwhile, 25 years after Amanda's death, the family continues to remember her. She left behind her mother, grandmother and her brother Chad, who was three years old at the time. A close friend of the family sadly recalled that Amanda's mother, Stephanie *"Monda"* Newton was never the same after her death. Even though she was initially treated by a counsellor, she took Amanda's death very hard, and lived and died a sad harrowing death a few years later.

Author's note: A decision was made not to use the name of the convicted person in this matter, as he has since returned to society and has successfully reintegrated as a productive member of society.

CRIME SCENE DO NOT CROSS

CHAPTER TWELVE

The Unsolved Murder of Gillian Bayne

G illian Alisha Bayne, or *Gill* as she was affec-
tionately called, was a very special child.
Special because she only weighed 2 ½ pounds
at birth, having been born prematurely while
her mother Thelma was seven months' pregnant. Her mother's water broke early and after
six weeks of hospitalisation, Thelma was finally
able to deliver Gillian by caesarian section on
July 16th, 1978. Gillian was so tiny she could fit
snugly into her mother's hand.

Gillian, the last of three daughters of Erskine, a
teacher, and Thelma, a nurse, spent two months
in the neonatal care of the Queen Elizabeth
Hospital. Her premature birth resulted in other
health issues, including underdeveloped lungs
and she would wheeze often.

Gillian Bayne

Thelma took a year off from work to take care of Gillian, with the "excellent
assistance" of Esther Archer, pediatrician. Despite her initial setbacks at birth, Gill
eventually grew out of the wheezing, her lungs developed and she progressed and
grew into a beautiful young lady.

Gill remained a very slim and petite young lady because of her early entrance
into the world; however, she excelled in every aspect of her life. She was intelligent,
creative and a great cook and baker. She spent her formative years at St Martins,
Mangrove, then passed the 11 plus exam where she entered Roebuck Secondary
School in 1989. And, says Thelma, "she did very well at Roebuck". She excelled in
her class, coming first in form all the time and received several awards. She was
involved with several clubs – Key Club, dancing club, and was very active in the
church and youth groups. Gillian loved to model and joined a modelling group
which was named 'Key Impulse'.

According to her peers, she was always a very quiet, friendly and polite person.
She never let anything bother her. She made friends easily and her teacher spoke
highly of her. She continued to graduate through the school, always maintaining
good grades.

She left Roebuck Secondary in July, 1995 and attended the Barbados Community
College in September 1995, where she entered the Science Department. Whilst
at the Barbados Community College, she ran for president in the Student Guild
Committee but was not elected. She however, continued to display leadership and
stayed active in her social life.

In addition to her love for cooking and baking, she was always a clean and tidy
person. Her mother recalled that one morning she came down the stairs to see

Gillian whipping up hamburgers in the kitchen with a cloth covering her arm. She told her mom that she didn't want any of the ingredients splashing on her body.

Thelma recalled Gillian as being a very fussy girl. From the age of nine when she started cooking, she would make her own breakfast, and she made some lovely fishcakes.

"We also had rules set down in the house. There was no timetable as such, but Gillian knew what she had to do on Saturday mornings in terms of cleaning – her bedroom and the dining room.

"Spick and span – she would clean the chandelier, take off the table cloth and put it to air, polish the table; that was her job every Saturday morning; that was her domain.

Thelma and her daughter had a loving relationship, and Gillian would always stay in touch with her mom, even on those long shifts at the hospital. "In those days, there was no cell phone, mainly beepers," said Thelma. "She would message or beep me on the beeper just to check in on me. We had a very close relationship," Thelma recalled sadly.

"Gillian would come to the Queen Elizabeth Hospital and sit in the lobby and do her homework after school," said Thelma. Everyone on the wards knew Gillian, and would admirably observe her sitting quietly waiting on her mom. When approaching the hospital, the nurses would say, "Sister Bayne, ya little queen coming."

Thelma believed that if she had continued studying, Gillian would have been a scholarship student. "She always wanted to do medicine; it was Gill's dream to be a pediatrician, and I tried my best to help her to have a good education so that she could achieve that goal."

Thelma explained that "Because Dr Archer (Gillian's pediatrician) did so much for her, she really wanted to go out and be there for babies. Every baby she would want to cuddle and play with it. Whenever we visited friends, she would always show interest in babies if there were any around. She really had a love for babies, and she told me 'Mum, someday I am going to be a pediatrician'."

Sadly, as fate would have it, that was not to be.

Gillian goes missing

It was the summer of 1996. Gillian was keen to be on summer break and was relaxing at home on August 12th. Her boyfriend of 14 months, 'M'*, was going overseas the next day (the 13th of August) and they were to spend the day together.

That morning began like any other morning. Gillian's older sister, Alison left home for work early for her 7 a.m. shift, leaving Gillian in bed. She made contact with Gillian later in the day, and they had light banter.

About 11 o'clock that morning, Gillian was speaking to her boyfriend 'M' on the phone. He told her that he had to go to Bridgetown and wanted her to come along as he wanted to do some shopping. He was moving to the USA to study. He was told that she had some chores to do and to call back later.

He called back some time between 1:00 and 2:00 pm. and was told that she could not go. However, she called him back around half an hour later and told him to come for her immediately.

About 2:00 p.m., Gillian's father Erskine left home to go by a brother, telling her that he would not be back until after 7:00 pm. According to police reports, Erskine left Gillian at home doing domestic chores. Gillian told her father she would not be home as she had made plans to go by 'M' at Mangrove.

Sometime after Erskine left home, 'M' arrived in his mother's car, along with his two-year-old cousin, and sounded the horn to indicate to Gillian that he was waiting for her. According to 'M', she came to the balcony and appeared surprised at his arrival and told him to give her ten minutes, as she was vacuuming. She then went into the house and he heard a sound as if she had resumed vacuuming. He remained outside for about 15 minutes and during that time, he sounded the horn several times as his little cousin was becoming restless.

'M' then left and headed to the service station at Kirtons in St Philip where he purchased gas and oil for the car. After leaving the service station, he returned to Gillian's house and sounded the horn. She appeared at the window, wearing a white bath towel and indicated to him that he should go on as she would keep him back. On hearing this, he left and went into Bridgetown.

Around 6:45 p.m., when 'M' returned from Bridgetown, he went to Gillian's house, but the house was in darkness. To him, it appeared that no one was at home and he left and went home.

Gillian's father returned home later and found the house in darkness. The back door was closed, but not locked. Everything was intact, except when he went to Gillian's bedroom and found the sheets dragged from the bed and the pillows on the floor. He thought nothing odd about it and went back downstairs.

About 8:00 p.m., 'M' called Gillian's residence enquiring for her, and Erskine told him that she was not at home. According to police reports, Erskine believed then that she was by her friend Althea.

An hour later, Gillian's aunt arrived at the residence as she usually slept over there since her residence had been burglarised on a previous occasion. She usually slept in Gillian's bedroom. On the night of Gillian's disappearance, she went upstairs to Gillian's bedroom, made up the bed and went to sleep.

During the night, 'M' called several times and was told each time that she was not at home. He also called Gillian's friend Althea and was also told that she was not there.

About 2:45 a.m, Erskine who had fallen asleep in the living room, awoke and made a check on the door and realised that the night latch was on. He was of the opinion that everyone was inside, as the person who last enters has the responsibility of putting on the latch. He went upstairs, and on checking Gillian's bedroom, realised that she was not there.

He woke Alison around this time, asking for Gillian, who then called Gillian's boyfriend to enquire where she was. After she was told that Gillian was not there and 'M' was in bed, Erskine made enquiries at some of Gillian's friends and at family members. After none of them reported knowing Gillian's whereabouts, Erskine became alarmed, and spoke with his brothers about Gillian's absence from home. They went by her boyfriend who by now was just as mystified about her disappearance, searched beaches for her, and after coming up empty-handed, they decided to report the matter to the police. When he came back home, Erskine then noticed what appeared to be Gillian's footprint in the vegetable garden behind his home, leading to a cane ground north of his home.

At this time, her mother Thelma was in Boston in the United States studying for her Masters in Public Health. "We would talk almost every day on the phone," she said. Gillian last spoke to her mother around 9 p.m. on Sunday, August 11th, 1996.

On the night of Monday, August 12th, 1996, the alarm was raised that Gillian was missing. Thelma was in class attending lectures on Tuesday, August 13th when the secretary of the Department came to the classroom and informed her that there was a call from Barbados from her family. With trepidation, Thelma went to the office, and was given the news no mother wants to hear.

"Mom," her middle daughter Alison said gravely. "We can't find Gillian."

"What do you mean?" said Thelma.

"She hasn't come home," said Alison._

Thelma noted that right there and then, her maternal instincts told her that Gillian was dead. "I just automatically knew it. I even told my professor that somebody had to have killed her." She packed and left for Barbados the Wednesday.

Gillian was at home alone during the day when she was allegedly abducted by a man. Reports indicated that Gillian was kidnapped from her home by a tall, slim young man, his arm around her shoulders, and was last seen near the Mill Wall of Kirtons, St Philip heading to a wooded area and wearing a white T-shirt and a blue pair of shorts. She was apparently seen being pulled by this man.

Thelma was met at the airport by Inspector Mark Thompson (now deceased) along with Mrs Beverly Arthur, then wife of Prime Minister Owen Arthur. When they arrived at the house, there were a lot of people there. By then, search parties including Gillian's relatives combed many St Philip districts for some trace of Gillian.

On arrival at the house, Thelma immediately noticed footsteps leading from the side door where canes were leading up to the low guard wall surrounding their home. She observed a track where the perpetrator had apparently traversed.

By Thursday, August 15th, 1996, the news had broken and the media was alerted. Headlines sprawled pictures and coverage. Gillian Bayne was missing. Where was she? At the time, Thelma made an impassioned appeal for Gillian's safe return.

"All I want to say is that whoever is out there, I am appealing for everybody's help... to help me find her alive. I want her back safely."

Interestingly at the time, police who were on the scene, according to newspaper reports, said so far they had not found any evidence to support an abduction theory.

In the Friday newspaper of August 16th, there was still no clue as to where Gillian was. It was reported that all of Barbados was mobilised into a massive search party as efforts intensified to find darling Gill. From daybreak, friends, family and well-wishers from St Philip and other parishes met at the Old Mill Wall near Kirton's in St Philip, where Gillian was last seen, to thoroughly comb the heavily wood 30 acres of agricultural lands looking for any sign of the missing teenager.

Lieutenant Colonel Clarence Gittens indicated that the Barbados Defence Force was ready and waiting if required to assist in the search.

Sniffer dogs which were being used in the search for Gillian, picked up a scent about 100 yards from an abandoned plant nursery. Hope disappeared when the scent was lost near an area which was wet and mucky from recent rains (*Advocate newspaper, Friday August 16th, 1996*).

One of Gillian's sisters, Shelly, who was residing in the USA, flew in on the Thursday to be with her family. Shelly joined residents and well-wishers who continued an around the clock vigil at the home of Erskine and Thelma Bayne.

Meanwhile, the search intensified and continued. One resident of the area who helped police comb the woodland, explained that there were several deep wells on the former sugar plantation. He was among the last persons to see 18-year-old Gillian alive when he sold her a newspaper on the Monday morning. He told the Advocate newspaper that the search had taken in part of Sterling Plantation near Sterling's children home.

A series of events before Gillian goes missing

It is worthy to note that a few strange occurrences happened just before Gillian disappeared. One of the dogs belonging to the family, Raydon, had been poisoned, and no one knew why this had happened. However, another dog was in the house when she was taken. The neighbours heard the dog barking the entire afternoon at the Baynes', but they thought nothing of it. In addition, two years prior, there had been a report of a burglary at the Bayne residence; the police never arrested anyone for the burglary.

Body of a girl found in a well

As the entire island waited with a collective breath for Gillian's disappearance to end in good news, the five-day search for Gillian ended somewhat in doubt on Friday, August 16th, 1996 when just before 9:00 am, the alarm was raised that a scent was picked up in a well off Groves Plantation in St Philip, a mile from Gillian's home.

Shortly before 9:00 a.m, a badly decomposed body of a female was spotted in the bottom of a 70 foot well. Gillian's family, the search team and other well-wishers were praying and holding on to hope that this body was not their darling Gill. However, it was widely speculated that it was indeed Gillian. The bloated body, clad in a jean shorts and t-shirt, similar to the clothes Gillian was last seen in before she disappeared was reported as unrecognisable, mangled by heat and the water. Moreover, there were no other persons missing in Barbados at that time. The area was quickly cordoned off around 9:45 a.m.

Acting Assistant Commissioner of Crime, Charles Blades, who headed a search party of about 80 police officers and more than two dozen civilians from as early as 5:30 a.m. told reporters that a stench led them to the well where the body was found.

Half an hour later, around 10:10 a.m., Thelma was brought to the scene, and as word spread that a body was found, within the space of minutes, hundreds of onlookers arrived at the scene to witness the recovery of the body from the well.

Close to 11:00 a.m., the Head of the Anglican Church, Bishop Rufus Broome, Father Edward Gatherer and Rector of Holy Trinity Anthony Holder arrived at the scene to bring comfort to the family and friends of Gillian. Shortly after, the hospital administrator Andrew Watson arrived to lend support to the Bayne family.

It was around three hours later, around 11:55 a.m. when a wire basket which was to be used in the recovery of the body, and other equipment, were brought to the scene by personnel of the Barbados Fire Service. At noon, rope, ladders, masks and other equipment were prepared for the descent into the well. Half an hour later, retired Fire Officer Anderson William (now deceased) who came to offer his expertise, was assisted with his oxygen tank, mask and tools before his descent into the well.

Close to 30 minutes later, the fire service ladder was hauled back from the mouth of the well, as loud instructions could be heard being shouted by those in the recovery process. Shortly afterwards, fire officers and other personnel formed two lines as they hauled the rope from the well. Meanwhile, a vehicle belonging to Two Sons Funeral home arrived on the scene.

Around 1:40 p.m. another oxygen tank was removed from the fire tender and taken to the well. Five minutes later, around 1:45 p.m., Anderson Williams emerged from between the rows of canes, visibly exhaling. Fifteen minutes later, at 2:00 p.m., a basket was brought back out from the vicinity of the well. Reporters noted hearing murmurs of "she coming out" from persons near the scene. Immediately after, Williams and Barbados Defence Force soldiers who returned to the well, were washed down by Fire Service personnel. The process took nearly six hours before the body was retrieved from the well. The long delay in retrieving the body was due to inadequate equipment.

Around 2:00 p.m., police escorted Thelma and Erskine Bayne across the field and at the edge of rows of cane to identify the body. Twelve minutes later, a doctor on the scene gave Gillian's parents and other relatives details about the body. Blades said at the time that the body was too badly decomposed for even the parents to positively identify it. However, Thelma said that she knew immediately that it was indeed Gillian, as one of the feet was smaller than the other, and this was a unique characteristic of Gill. Blades also confirmed that four boulders were found on the body. He noted that a little water was also in the well.

Coroner Magistrate Shirley Clarke and Dr Belfield Brathwaite, who were also at the canefield in Sterling, pronounced the victim dead.

Hundreds of people converged in the field to get a glimpse of Gillian's body. The media reported that from mothers with babes in arms to those who barely had time to take out their curlers gathered in the vicinity of Sterling Plantation from early that morning.

When Gillian's body was eventually brought out of the well, some of her friends who were gathered in the crowd wept openly, sobbing loudly and hoping that it was not indeed their darling Gill.

Media reports that many prayed and some discussed angrily what they would do to someone who committed such a crime. They were loud suggestions that "these people so should get their necks popped."

In a later interview, Williams, the retired fireman who retrieved the body, told the press "it was a bit gruelling". He also recalled the moments while he was being lowered. "I was let down by a rope. The situation was that the few boulders and the body – the position – it was a bit tight for me to remove the stones alone – seeing as they were thrown afterwards."

Williams, retired at that time for some 11 years, also said when he saw the body, it was in a fetal position.

"It was just folded, just as it came up. The body was probably there for about two days. It was dressed in black jeans shorts and a shirt, barefoot. I would assume it was a woman because she had a lot of hair," he concluded.

Blades said police would be looking at all information available to them and continue their investigation and were hopeful that success would come quickly.

But it would be some time yet before any positive identification could be made on the remains found in the well. Dr K. Sree Ramulu, government forensic psychologist, explained that a dental records examination would be done by someone else in order to ascertain who was the female pulled from the well.

Anglican Bishop of Barbados Rufus Brome condemned the murder of Gillian as a "vicious act which shows the rottenness of the society".

"This is a part of the evilness and the sickness existing in the society. Sometimes we are very pretensive. Behind the thin layer of respectability within our society there is a lot of rottenness and vicious wickedness and this has surfaced in this kind of way," Bishop Brome said at the time.

Brome said that as a society we have to stop dealing with the symptoms and look at the real malady affecting the country, adding he could not imagine what would have motivated someone to carry out such a violent act. He said it was clear that the person would have to be possessed by something else other than the Spirit of God.

"We should be able to bring the person or persons to justice and deal with it swiftly. I condemn this most vicious crime on an innocent and young person's life being taken in that kind of way," the Bishop said.

Brome said that Barbadians must stop pointing the accusing finger at all the institutions and work together in an effort to find out what was wrong.

"The home, the church, the school, all our institutions must be able to work together for the good of the country and I still believe there is the need for a task force to look into the situation and try to deal with it," he added.

Bishop Bromes also said in an interview with the Advocate shortly after Gillian's murder, that Government needed to act immediately and look at the dangers associated with the public having access to the numerous wells scattered all over Barbados.

Calling for all open wells to be sealed, Bishop Brome said that Government and private land owners had a responsibility to ensure that wells were securely covered and did not endanger the general public.

Bromes believed that as long as wells remained uncovered, they were potentially dangerous.

However, then public relations officer for the Royal Barbados Police Force, Inspector Jeddar Robinson, said sealing wells would not deter people from disposing of corpses. He said that if all the island's wells were sealed off from public access, murderers or any other persons wishing to conceal bodies would simply find somewhere else. Robinson said that he was not sure if it would make a difference if wells were closed off because "people dump bodies anywhere" and irrespective of circumstances, the devastating effects of their discovery were just as traumatic for victims' families. Robinson also noted that a lot of wells were on private property making it the responsibility of the owners to seal wells to which the public had access.

Potential witnesses

Around 4:40 pm on the day Gillian went missing, a 12-year-old girl, who lived in the path between Gillian's house and the well, was at home in Kirtons babysitting her ten-month old sister, when she heard voices coming from the bushy area to the western side of her house. She saw two persons, a man holding a woman by her right hand coming from the area where she heard the voices. The man was about 5'10" and of dark complexion, medium built, with a medium sized head and long face. He had big ears and short knotty hair. He was wearing an orange coloured T-shirt and what appeared to be a blue or black pants. The two persons walked from the cartroad and turned left on to Kirtons #3. However, she said could not give a full description of the man and that she would be unable to identify him if she saw him again.

She spoke to her mother the day after Gillian went missing and deduced, after she heard about the missing girl, that it was Gillian she had seen walking with the man. However, she admitted that she had not paid any particular attention to her on that day.

That same day, around 4:20 p.m., Lynne of Kirtons, St Philip was on her way home from work when she saw two persons walking towards her at a distance. The man was holding the woman by her right hand with his left hand. The woman did not appear to be struggling, nor did they say anything. Lynne then saw them off on her left into a bushy area. On reaching the area where she saw the persons turned off, she made a check but did not see anyone. The man was of dark complexion and was wearing a black T-shirt. The woman was fair-skinned and was wearing a white T-shirt.

Yet another person from Kirtons was in his garden sometime during the evening when he saw a man and a woman in the distance walking towards Sterling Children's home, but he did not recognise who they were or what they were wearing.

Profiling the killer

Former criminal psychologist for the Royal Barbados Police Force, Miss Janice Farley, now deceased, prepared a profile of the offender who in her opinion, killed

Gillian based on 'inferences of behaviours exhibited from the crime scene'. In her report, Farley believed that the killer *may* have lived within walking distance, as "persons who commit abduction crimes normally commit the initial attack nearer to their home base than to the actual culminating point (in this case, the well)". She believed that the offender was more likely to have lived nearer to Kirtons than Sterling, St Philip. The well was more likely to be used to distance the offender from the initial criminal activity, which was Gillian's residence.

The killer also may (i)) have been arrested before since no fingerprints were found at the scene of the crime; (ii) more likely had returned to the well, and retraced his path because of the 'staging' of the scene; (iii) had lived closer to the victim's residence than the well; (iv) knew the area well, suggestive of being generally from the area.

She also believed that the person was exhibiting asocial psychopathic behaviour by the dropping of boulders on the body and seemingly ignoring the victim's pleading.

Farley stated that the taking of the victim away from the house seemed to be reactionary, impulsive behaviour. She noted that this was a panic and emotional response. At that stage, the offender was behaving irrationally.

The psychologist also noted that there was implied intimacy between the victim and the offender; this was indicative of the way he hugged the victim when in view of other persons.

She went on to say that the person exhibited behaviours expressive of the need to punish or chastise, stressing that this was not the first time the person would have done this (shown signs of that behaviour). The profiler believed that the killer was an authority person.

She stressed that the victim knew the person well, and there was a relationship that existed between them. She also trusted the person. She came to this conclusion because of Gillian's inability to struggle and her inability to shout.

Farley concluded that Gillian's murder was a confidence crime and an acquaintance murder. The killing seemed to be reactionary probably due to the victim's response (probably her threat to reveal his identity and what happened prior to leaving the house) the report said. She believed that the killing happened but was not intended, with the killer remorseful, guilty or frightened. It seemed, she said, like a situation that had probably gone wrong, and the motivation was maybe to hide a crime such as a sexual crime or a burglary. The initial act was to teach Gillian a lesson or frighten her.

The criminal psychologist had argued that the house should have been thoroughly examined for forensic evidence which would have supplied information where the police could have attempted to decipher a motive. She also argued that a time, date and event flow tracing of all the activities of the person(s) who might have last seen Gillian alive at the house should have been conducted and any discrepancies cleared up. It is unclear if this was done.

Meanwhile retired police Superintendent Jasper Watson said the assailant who murdered the woman found in the well would strike again "and I suspect it will be soon", he said at the time. Speaking to the *Barbados Advocate,* the former leading criminal analyst commented on the Gillian Bayne case, suggesting that whoever was responsible for her disappearance may kill again to camouflage the crime.

"Having studied the conduct of criminals for a number of years and having made my analysis, I believe the perpetrator needs to camouflage the crime with a similar or another crime, so attention would be turned away from him. When that happens, he slips..."

The retired superintendent also believed that the perpetrator possessed certain character traits – namely authoritative, intelligent and meticulous. He believed the perpetrator was at the time restless, mentally unstable and aggressive – keeping a close eye on the investigation via the media.

Final confirmation - it is Gillian Bayne

On August 21st, 1996, the family of Gillian had their worst fears realised when fingerprints positively identified Gillian after dentists were unable to make the positive identification. It was even suggested that Gillian may have been sexually molested and strangled, but neither that nor the exact cause of death of the 18-year-old were ever confirmed.

The final goodbye

Goodbye Gillian

Hundreds of people from all walks of life attended the thanksgiving service for a young lady who was taken much too soon. Tears filled the eyes of most who gathered to say goodbye to Gillian – the young, the old and those in between. Gillian's family, friends, school mates, neighbours, and general well-wishers turned out in their large numbers looking dazed and in disbelief that what unfolded in weeks prior was indeed reality or just a horrible nightmare. Sadly, it was no dream.

Well before the 3:00 p.m. start, Holy Trinity Anglican church was literally over-flowing. Inside, there was hardly a dry eye with sobs and cries adding to the already sombre mood of the service, according to Ryan Broome of the *Advocate*.

Students and administration staff from the Barbados Community College, where Gillian last went to school, wore sashes bearing college colours in honour of their friend and colleague. Principal of the BCC Norma Holder played the church organ during the rendition of a few hymns.

Gillian's former modelling group *'Key Impulse'* showed their solidarity by wearing black and white ribbons; while colleagues with whom Gillian attended the former Roebuck Secondary delivered an a capella rendition of 'Amazing Grace'.

As Gillian's coffin was slowly lowered, and the 'thud' of the gravel being shovelled on it filled the atmosphere, the loud mournful wails increased.

Gillian's father Erskine had to rush to the side of one of the children who was clearly overcome by grief, as she cried uncontrollably.

One year after Gillian's death, residents of Kirtons said that not a day went by that they did not think about Gillian's brutal murder. However, they clung to the hope that one day, her killer would be found. Despite assurances from the police that the case was still being investigated, and as time progressed, and no arrests were made, residents had all but concluded that no one would be brought to justice.

Then director of the St Philip-based Pure Referral Centre, Carl Padmore said "It is sad that a murder which has thrown a country into a state of grief, that no one has been brought to justice. I believe that someone or a group of persons know who has committed that sort of crime and are withholding that information from the police," he declared.

Padmore also charged that the lack of police protection for those persons giving evidence is preventing them from coming forward. He also made an appeal to the authorities not to let this die as another "unsolved mystery", and pleaded with anyone who could help to release any information which might assist them to solve this case.

Gillian's murder has stayed on the lips of Barbadians for decades after that sad summer of 1996. Many persons were interviewed, profiles of the killer created, and the case eventually grew cold. There were a few leads over the years, but they all led to no arrests.

The effects of Gill's death on her family

Today, 23 years after Gillian's murder, the family continues to grieve for and miss Gillian. Thelma's life almost came to a standstill after Gillian's death, and she had to seek continuous counselling for the past 20-plus years.

Thelma reflects on Gillian

Christmas time is hard. In an interview with the media in 2000, she remembered that Gillian's role was to dress up the house at Christmas time.

"Every time I attempted since then to put up that Christmas tree, a little voice in my head would tell me: 'You had better leave it; that's Gill's job.'

In an interview with Tony Vanderpool in 2001, Thelma while reflecting on that fateful day, felt that the situation might have been different had she been around.

"I was not there at the time. I went to do my Masters in Health Resources Administration but I was only able to complete half of a semester of the programme when I got the news and returned home from the USA." She never completed the programme.

She said to Vanderpool "Sometimes I tell myself, 'If I was here, maybe I would have been able to see things (that happened in my absence).

"If she had classes, I would stay at work late and I would wait for her instead of going to St Philip and returning."

Thelma also believes that whoever broke into the house in 1994 was the same person who was involved in Gillian's death.

"When we had that burglary, Gill was not here; she was in the United States. My other daughter was working and when she came home, she realised that the house was broken into. So she didn't bother to go in at all.

"Obviously the person would have to be scoping and watching the movements in the household. And Gillian was at a vulnerable age that people would look at her. Whoever it is, I am hoping that one day I will be able to ask him – why?"

Thelma is a little disappointed because she says those who are supposed to be investigating the crime have left her out in the cold.

"I feel from time to time they should come and give me some progress report. It is about two years now that I haven't seen or heard anything from anyone," she told Vanderpool in 2001.

She does not go back to Kirtons, and does not even like to visit St Philip. What is particularly painful is that no one has ever been arrested for Gillian's murder, and the case has long gone cold. The horrific images of a bloated mangled body haunt her to this day, and she will not rest until she learns who killed Gillian.

Thelma is resolute in her belief that she knows who killed Gillian, and believes that he is currently incarcerated for another serious matter. Ironically, he was one of many persons questioned by the police shortly after Gillian's murder. She has gone public with her belief as well. When asked what would bring closure to her, Thelma responded: "I am a Christian, and the Christian thing to do, I guess, is to forgive him. But I would like him [the murderer] to come out and admit to Barbadians that he is responsible for Gillian's death. I just want to ask [him] 'what did Gillian do you? What would possess you to pick up Gillian barefooted and carry her so far away from her home?'"

The Bayne family, friends of Gillian, and indeed Barbados still await the answers to those questions.

* To protect the innocent, instead of the name of Gillian's boyfriend the letter 'M' was used.

CRIME SCENE DO NOT CROSS

CHAPTER THIRTEEN

Revenge Turned Deadly

A nna Druizhinina, 16 years of age, was born in Russia but came to Barbados at the age of seven with her parents Larissa and John Jackson. John, who lived in Barbados for more than 30 years, was Anna's stepfather. One day after celebrating her 16th birthday, she was hanged from a rafter in the Jackson's home at Palmers Plantation, St John. Medical reports indicated that she died from ligature strangulation. The gruesome death was a "revenge killing" by Teerath Persaud, 44, an ex-employee of her step father's business who three months earlier had been shot in the arm by John, after they got into an altercation following the disappearance of Bds $100,000.00 from John's wholesale business So-Lo Wholesalers in Black Rock, St Michael.

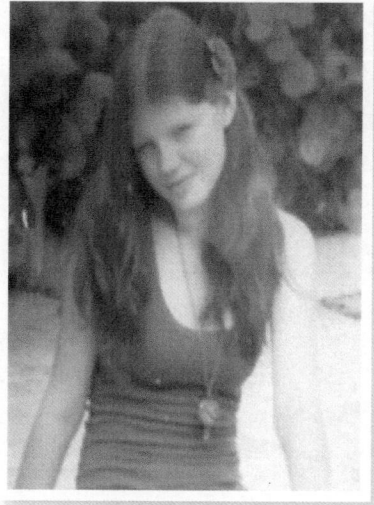

Anna Druizhinina

Teerath Persaud worked as an agricultural worker at Palmers Plantation in St. Philip which was owned by John Jackson. John said that he helped Persaud to build his house, and even before that, helped him in getting his family to Barbados. However, there were stories of the family stealing from what they were growing on John's farm and John released him. However, Persaud begged for his job back and he took him back.

Mr Persaud was transferred from the Palmers Plantation and allowed to stay in an apartment at his employer's Black Rock business rent-free, where he looked after the So-Lo business as a caretaker, watchman and sometimes assisted in the business.

Sometime before November 2008, a considerable sum of money went missing from Mrs Jackson's bag. There was a confrontation between Mr Jackson and Mr Persaud, which resulted in Mr Persaud being shot in the left shoulder. Mr Jackson alleged that Persaud charged at him with a knife after their confrontation, and he retaliated by shooting him in the shoulder. However, Jackson was charged by the police with causing serious bodily harm to Mr Persaud, while Persaud was never charged with anything. Persaud's employment was terminated, and he took up residence at Blades Hill in St Philip.

On November 8th, 2008, the Jacksons went to work at the Black Rock business leaving their daughter Anna at home at Palmers Plantation to do her Saturday chores.

Little did they know that Persaud, who had babysat for Anna for several years and knew the house inside out, had just been released from the hospital and had rented a room at a house a short distance away from their home. He had hired Christopher McCollin, a 26-year-old, who was described as a "simpleton", to help him in his dastardly crime by telling him that he was going to commit a robbery. Jackson, in an interview with the author, alleged that the nurses in the hospital heard Persaud say he was going to kill Jackson and his entire family, but this could not be substantiated.

Later that day, Persaud and his co-accused McCollin went to the residence with the intention to steal. The two entered the house around 5:30 p.m. and immediately started working on Anna.

Persaud's knowledge of the area and his familiarity with the Jackson's dogs meant that he and the co-accused encountered no difficulty in gaining entry to the residence. On entering the home, they encountered Anna, who started to scream. McCollin seized her on the balcony and bound her feet, and tied her arms behind her back with electric wire which had been retrieved by Persaud from a room downstairs. He then tied a towel around her face to silence her screams. Persaud watched as McCollin used a long piece of wire to make a draw knot which he put around her neck, threw the other end over a beam in the ceiling and made Anna stand on a paint can and bucket, one on top of the other. The can and bucket had been retrieved from elsewhere in the house by Persaud. She was left precariously perched on these containers whilst McCollin searched the house looking for items to steal and Persaud waited on the balcony.

After searching the house "for a very long time," McCollin returned to the balcony and informed Persaud that Anna had fallen or jumped off the bucket and tin. According to John, instead of trying to save her, Persaud said to leave her alone. "They stood and watched her die," said John.

Court documents showed that McCollin took the body down and placed it on a bed. McCollin rested on the balcony for some time and then told Persaud that he was going downstairs to look for gasoline. He returned to the bedroom with the gasoline and set fire to the room. On seeing the headlights of the Jackson's car coming into the entrance to the Palmers Plantation, Persaud ran downstairs and made good his escape.

Mr Jackson found his home on fire and later discovered his daughter's body.

According to the Nation newspaper, the couple said they would never forget the night when they returned home around 11:30 p.m. to find Anna's lifeless body on her bed, her arms and feet bound behind her back and a kitchen towel tied around her neck. They were oblivious to what was going to greet them until they actually were in the house and noticed a fire at the back of the house.

It was then that they made the grisly discovery. While Larissa ran to the back of the house, John headed for Anna's bedroom. Even though the lights were off, he saw flames coming from the ground by the carpet. John told *Nation* reporter, Maria Bradshaw in his interview that while stamping out the flames, he saw Anna's body on the bed, and started shouting to her. He shouted, 'Anna, what are you doing?', but there was no answer, so he ran to the body, touching Anna, but got no response. It was only then that he noticed that she was bound and gagged face down. "When I turned her over there was blood in her eyes. I put her face against mine and she was still warm but I knew she was dead.

"I scooped her up in my arms, and started crying 'No, not Anna,'" John cried.

John told Maria that he knew there and then who had killed his step daughter. He trembled uncontrollably as Larissa ran to the room and he told her that Anna, her only child, was dead.

"Larissa ran into the room screaming that the house was on fire, but all I could do was hug Anna and cry. I said, 'Larissa, they've killed her; they've killed Anna', he told the journalist in his exclusive interview.

"Larissa was in a trance, and then she started running around the bed like a mad woman. She just went crazy. I sat with Anna in my arms and I asked God to just let me die – let the house burn down. I just wanted to die.

"You have no idea reliving the horrible experience of seeing your daughter with blood in her eyes laying there bound and helpless," said John. "I could hear the blood bubbling in Anna's throat after trying to give her mouth to mouth," cried John.

He also said that the sheet around her bed was soaked in kerosene oil. If John had not gone to the room in time, the flames from the carpet would have caught the bed and he would have been greeted with a burning inferno of Anna's body. "They had two barrels with diesel and petrol with the intention to light the entire place. This was done to punish me," said John.

John called the Barbados Fire Service and the police and told them: "Teereth did this."

Teereth Persaud

That very night, Persaud was taken into custody. He gave a written statement to police officers setting out in detail the events that had transpired. He stated that his co-accused, McCollin wanted to do landscaping work and he had informed him that Mr. Jackson had tools at his home which they could steal. He advised McCollin that Saturday would be the best day to steal the items as no one would be home.

Teereth Persaud

McCollin was also arrested and charged. He too gave a statement to police officers, confessing to the offence and that statement was accepted by the Director of Pubic Prosecutions as the basis for his sentencing. However, the account by McCollin differed markedly from that of Persaud. According to McCollin, Persaud had told him that Mr Jackson had shot him and that he wanted to get back at him. McCollin said that Persaud was the primary actor in grabbing the deceased as she began to scream, and it was Persaud who went in search of wire to tie her up. McCollin, however, admitted to tying her hands behind her back and taking a cloth from the kitchen and tying it around her face. He said that it was Persaud who tied a piece of wire around the Anna's neck and pulled at it so that "it closed in around her neck [and that] it was lifting her off the ground." Persaud also told him to take Anna to the top of the staircase and "string her up." McCollin then "stood on the bannister and threw the wire over a rafter and wrapped it around the bannister rail."

Persaud then suggested that they put her to stand on cans and produced the cans on which they hoisted her. McCollin said that Anna asked if they were going to kill her and he told her not if he had anything to do with it. He said that after realising that Anna had died he took her down and placed her on the bed. He cried because he could not believe he was "in this situation." He said Persaud was the one who suggested that they set the room on fire.

According to pathologist Dr Stephen Jones who carried out the post mortem examination, death was caused by ligature strangulation.

John told the **SUNDAY SUN** that Persaud, who worked as a security officer at So-Lo, knew that Anna had celebrated her birthday the day before and that her biological father had hanged himself in the same manner when Anna was just a toddler. "She pleaded for her life. She told him, 'Please don't kill me like this, my daddy [John] will give you anything you want,' but he stuffed a cloth in her mouth to stop her from screaming. He did this to hurt Larissa. He knew Larissa was devastated at the way Anna's father had died and he wanted her to feel it all over again."

As to the fire at the back of the house, John said Persaud also knew that it was his labour of love for Larissa; that he had worked on it for five years and it was finally completed. "He knew it was my labour of love and he started the fire there. He did not burn the house to hide any evidence as he told the police. He started the fire at the back of the house where I had built this beautiful room for Larissa," he cried.

John also believed that Anna was not the only one who was supposed to die that day. According to Persaud's statement, when they reached home he was still there hiding behind a door with John's loaded speargun in his hand. Persaud pulled the trigger, but the gun jammed.

John said, "They entered the house at 5:30 p.m. and waited for five hours until we got home at 11:30. They sat on our balcony drinking drinks from our refrigerator while Anna was inside the house hanging. When they saw our headlights approaching, they set the house on fire, put Anna on the bed, soaked it with kerosene oil and lit it so that we could come in and see her body in flames."

They said McCollin's statement was proof enough that Persaud's sole intent was murder. He told the court: "In no way I wanted her to die. I tried my best to prevent it but I couldn't do anything about it. I also feared for my life, but I saw the anger go through him [Persaud]. I tried my best."

The couple was also shocked when they later discovered that the two men were hiding in the house the whole time.

In the plea in mitigation, Andrew Pilgrim Q.C. submitted that the co-accused "was led by Persaud and that he was therefore definitely the secondary party." He said that his only interest was to "get some weed whackers and so from this place" and that "his motive at the highest would have been theft."

On August 8th, 2010, Justice Worrell found that the case warranted the imposition of a custodial sentence because of the seriousness of the offence which was caused by the reckless actions of McCollin and Persaud, which took place in the victim's home. He said it was "quite clear that this young lady was tied up and left, more or less, to balance on paint cans." He said that "that in itself must have been a traumatic exercise to undergo". He noted that "the end result" was that "a person of 16 years of age, lost her life due to recklessness or reckless disregard for the sanctity not only of the home, but also of the sanctity of human life." It was a "senseless, totally mindless tragic act," said Justice Worrell. The Judge said that the starting point for a sentence of imprisonment should be 20 years.

He thereafter considered the mitigating circumstances of the case, that is, an early guilty plea, the co-accused's remorse, his clean record, his age (26 years old at the time of the offence) and conduct in his community. The Judge therefore sentenced McCollin to 16 years' imprisonment and ordered time spent on remand for 20 months to be deducted.

Persaud was arraigned on September 11th, 2012 and he entered a plea of not guilty to murder. At the start of trial on October 22nd, 2012, he pleaded not guilty to murder but guilty to manslaughter. In advance of the trial date, his intention to enter this plea had been communicated to the DPP. The DPP accepted his plea, and his statement to the police was also read into evidence. In his plea in mitigation, his attorney, Mr A. Boardi, suggested that a sentence of ten years would be appropriate considering all the mitigating factors.

The judge, Justice Maureen Crane-Scott, found that this was a serious case of manslaughter on the borderline of murder with numerous aggravating factors. She said that while no gun or intrinsically dangerous weapon was used, the facts showed that the victim's life was not "taken from her with a flash of a gun or thrust of a knife" but her death "was no quick and sudden death."

She found that the matter was one that warranted a custodial sentence because: (a) the offence was committed in the home of Persaud's former employer; (b) after being surprised by the victim's presence they proceeded to embark on "a most bizarre and reckless plan to silence her"; (c) Persaud stood and watched as McCollin tied up the victim, Anna and covered her face; (d) Persaud had knowledge of the house and its contents and could, at the request of the co-accused, locate certain items; (e) although no gun or intrinsically dangerous weapon was used, the manner in which Anna was treated including being placed to stand precariously on the containers with a noose around her neck "showed that she suffered a thousand deaths before her inevitable strangulation."; (f) the seriousness of the offence; (g) Persaud's lack of concern following the news that she had fallen from the cans; (h) Persaud failed to actively discourage the co-accused McCollin from setting fire to the house; and (i) Persaud personally knew the victim and her parents.

The judge found the conduct of Persaud particularly callous and reprehensible and held that a reasonable starting point would therefore be 30 years. The judge held that Persaud's guilty plea would warrant a reduction of four years. Persaud's clean record up to the date of the offence, his cooperation with the police in making an oral and written statement upon arrest as well as his remorse since the pre-sentence report also led to the discount of another year. Although informed that the co-accused McCollin had been sentenced to 16 years, the judge sentenced Persaud to 25 years' imprisonment with a discount of four years and 26 days for time spent on remand.

As far as John and Larissa Jackson were concerned, it was the most horrific form of punishment another human being could give them. "He wanted to cause us the maximum amount of pain," wrote John in a lengthy letter to the SUNDAY SUN following Persaud's sentence and who had since returned to England. "If this is not murder, then tell me what is?" he asked.

Persaud appealed to the Court of Appeal on the basis that the sentence was manifestly excessive because he received a sentence that was nine years longer than his co-accused whom the DPP accepted to be the primary aggressor in the commission of the offence.

The Court of Appeal comprising of Sir Marston Gibson CJ, Justices of Appeal Burgess and Goodridge dismissed the appeal in the written judgment of Justice of Appeal Goodridge. The court held that disparity in sentences, by itself, was not a ground for reducing a sentence.

The Court of Appeal also found no fault with the judge's comment that the Appellant was equally or more culpable than his co-accused. The Appellant had previously enjoyed the confidence of the family, was familiar with the dogs and the surrounding and knew the family's habits to the extent that he was fully aware of their goings and comings. Additionally, the court found that the judge's assessment that the Appellant's actions displayed a lack of concern for the deceased was a fair assessment.

Persaud continued to appeal, this time to the Caribbean Court of Justice. In Persaud's appeal to the CCJ, filed on September 26th, 2017, Persaud listed some nine grounds of appeal, but these were essentially that (a) his sentence lacked parity with that of the co-accused and (b) his sentence was excessive because of the high starting point taken by the judge and her misapplication of the aggravating and mitigating factors.

The CCJ ruled that they found that the fact that the Appellant personally knew the victim and her parents and the attendant circumstances surrounding his familiarity with the family to be a serious aggravating factor. The Appellant's personal knowledge and past relationship with the deceased and her parents rendered his actions an especially reprehensible breach of trust towards the deceased whom he had known from the time she was a little girl.

Putting to one side the discount for the guilty plea, which was dealt with separately, they agreed with the judge in the Court of Appeal that there were mitigating factors in favour of the Appellant. These were that he had no record of previous offences, cooperated with the police investigations by making oral as well as written statements and his expression of remorse. However, these were outweighed by the aggravating factors peculiar to the Appellant, particularly his breach of trust.

Despite this, the CCJ reduced Persaud's sentence to 18 years, including time spent on remand. The CCJ, in their judgement stated: -

"Considering the appropriate sentence for the Appellant we considered that the starting point of 25 years should be adjusted upwards by two years on the basis of the balancing of the aggravating and mitigating factors to produce a notional term of 27 years. A discount of one-third (nine years) for the Appellant's early guilty plea is appropriate resulting in a term of 18 years. We consider that a term of 18 years is justifiable even with consideration of the parity principle given the significant breach of trust committed by the Appellant.

"From this notion a term of 18 years the full period of four years and 26 days spent on remand must be deducted leaving an actual term of 13 years and 339 days.

"The sentence of 25 years' imprisonment imposed on the Appellant is set aside and the Court substitutes pursuant to section 14 of the Criminal Appeal Act Cap 113A a sentence of 13 years and 339 days to run from the original date of sentence, December 11, 2012."

In a newspaper article headline entitled *"Grieving all over again for Anna"*, the Jacksons said that they were heartbroken at the reduction of the sentence for Persaud, whom they perceived as the main instigator of the murder of their daughter. In an interview from their home in Spain, John said after the 2008 crime, he thought her killers would receive the maximum sentence.

Anna with her mother Larissa in happier times

"After what he [Persaud] did I thought there would not be any question of it. To take a little girl's life, an innocent child just 16 – to torture her; to degrade her. How could I think anything otherwise than they would throw the book at these people?

Anna in happier times

"I knew Persaud would never get hanged because Barbados doesn't hang people, but I truly expected, with the abhorrence of normal human beings against such an animal that would just torture and kill a little girl, there would be no question in anybody's mind this man needs locking up forever."

A few years after Anna's death the heartbroken couple left Barbados for England, John's birthplace after Larissa got critically sick.

"We lost everything. I worked all of my life at Palmers farming before I opened the store. Everything I worked for disappeared the day we got on a plane and left Barbados five years ago," said John, who lived in Barbados for 35 years.

John told Maria Bradshaw in his interview with the **Nation** that the crime had taken a toll on Larissa, 46, a Russian nurse whom he met and married when Anna, her only child, was seven years old. She developed Parkinson's disease after the murder.

"At the moment she's virtually disabled and she can only stay alive on drugs," Jackson said of his wife.

"She needed brain surgery and she couldn't get it because of our financial situation so they did an operation and fit her with an electronic part so now she gets continuous medication pumped into her body with a tube."

He said that he suffered from traumatic shock syndrome. He has partially lost his voice and had to get voice training.

John is adamant that the criminal justice system was against him going back to a bitter child custody case thirty-five years prior to Anna's murder. He said that it was a matter of "ongoing persecution" by the judiciary and the police that started when he, as a British citizen was challenged because he fought to keep his biological daughter in Barbados after a court battle with his daughter's mom that became an international case. "I was treated like a criminal on at least three occasions," John stressed. He is adamant that because he brought the case to international attention, that he became the target of the system and even believed that everything, including the sentence of Persaud, the fact that he, John, was charged for serious bodily harm, and not Persaud, and prior minor brush-ins were all calculated and intentional due to the decades old court battle.

Persaud was released from Her Majesty's Prison, Dodds on May 23rd, 2003 while McCollin was released in August 2022.

Pearl Cornelius

Shanna Griffith

Kellisha Olliviere

Tiffany Harding

Nikita Belgrave

Kelly-Ann Welch

CRIME SCENE DO NOT CROSS

CHAPTER FOURTEEN

Of Robbery, Arson and Murder: Campus Trendz

Pearl Cornelius   Shanna Griffith   Kellisha Olliviere

Tiffany Harding   Nikita Belgrave   Kelly-Ann Welch

One of the most horrifying murders that sparked much anger and debate from the Barbadian public was that of six young women, ages 18 to 26, which changed the lives of their friends and loved ones forever.

On September 3rd, 2010, Nikita Belgrave, Pearl Cornelius, Shanna Griffith, Tiffany Harding, Kellishaw Ollivierre and Kelly-Ann Welch died when the clothing store they were in, was firebombed by robbers.

This chapter is centred around that robbery and firebombing as well as the firebombing of another business by the same perpetrators in 2010.

The first robbery occurred in August, 2010 at Chicken Galore, a depot which sells chicken and chicken by-products in Bank Hall, St Michael. Jamar and his partner Renaldo, firebombed the depot with a Molotov cocktail. Renaldo Alleyne posed as a customer. The building was razed to the ground but thankfully no one was physically hurt.

The second robbery occurred three weeks later on September 3rd at Campus Trendz, a clothing store in Tudor Street in the City of Bridgetown. Using similar modus operandi, both Renaldo and Jamar entered the clothing store and robbed the store, with Renaldo throwing two Molotov cocktails into the store. However, unlike the first incident, the owner was stabbed by Jamar and the throwing of the Molotov cocktails resulted in the deaths of Tiffany Harding, Pearl Cornelius, Kellishaw Ollivierre, Shana Griffith, Kelly Ann Welch and Nikkita Belgrave.

The two men were convicted of manslaughter and murder. On June 1st 2011, Alleyne pleaded not guilty to murder but admitted to manslaughter. However, Bynoe decided to go to trial and pleaded not guilty to either murder or manslaughter.

On August 15th 2012, Madame Justice Elneth Kentish ruled that Renaldo Anderson Alleyne would spend the rest of his life behind bars. Jamar decided to take his case to trial and was found guilty of murder and sentenced to hang in July 2016. He had since appealed his sentence, but lost the appeal.

This chapter looks at the lives of the perpetrators; their upbringing, criminal and deviant histories, the planning and execution of their robberies, how they were caught and their views on the crimes they committed. It will then examine the lives of the victims, including those who survived and whose lives have been forever changed by these crimes.

THE PERPETRATORS

"I believe now is the time to tell the story. Full time. I am giving the full details because I desperately want to tell somebody about it because I do not feel good about the crime I committed". – Renaldo Alleyne, April 2017

RENALDO ALLEYNE

Renaldo "Naldo" Alleyne was born on June 9th, 1989. The fourth of five children - three brothers and one sister, Renaldo was the unassuming one of the siblings. He was from Prescod Bottom, an urban community on the outskirts of Bridgetown, where he lived all of his life with his parents Charles and Deborah, and two of his siblings. At the time of the Campus Trendz tragedy, he was 21 years old.

Renaldo attended Carrington's Primary School and Alleyne Secondary School, where he received no O'Level qualifications. He repeated his 2nd year at secondary school, because of family issues which led to a prolonged absence from school. "Me, my mother and my brother went by a family member for a few months due to an issue at home. I wasn't going to school. My mother was working and finances and distance were an issue," said Renaldo. He left school at 17 years old.

After leaving school, he was employed at KFC, Oistins, but was laid off from this job. He attended skills

Renaldo Alleyne

training doing cupboard construction. He finished the course and was hired at Regal Furniture, Brighton, St Michael, where he was employed for a year but was dismissed for late attendance and for having a dispute with his boss. He worked part-time servicing kitchens with Grand G Sales and Services Inc.

He was not working at the time of the tragedy. Prior, he was working at Lavada's Laundry and had just left working with them as, according to him, he had "problems with being given demands."

Renaldo said he stopped going to church in secondary school. "I stopped myself," he said. "I said I don't need this."

According to him, "I never mixed up with people that sorta way." He would lime on the block but was relatively quiet among the guys, and was not known as one to get into trouble. He would however hustle in the drug business, selling marijuana, cocaine, 'fanta' and cigarettes.

Renaldo always knew Jamar but initially never mixed with him. He was mainly the friend of Jamar's uncle. He then became friendly with Jamar through said uncle who basically introduced them to each other. "Me and Jamar spirit just meet," he said. "We are both June born, and seven days apart." They would talk about girls, smoke marijuana and lime together.

Criminal history

Renaldo admitted to committing robberies before the tragedy where he targeted tourists. He would rob them with a knife. He sought to explain why he used knives to commit robberies. "I preferred knives to guns," said Renaldo. "Guns keep too much noise and make an explosion, but knives are silent."

Product of the environment?

He blamed his criminal activity on being young and naïve, and most importantly his environment. "I was raised in a ghetto environment," Renaldo said. "All I saw was robberies and crime." He said he saw robberies on the block he would hang out on, and even admitted that he too was a victim of robberies. "A gun was stuck to my belly already," he said. According to him, robbers stole "weed, money and gold" from the men on the block.

Renaldo was exposed to a lot of violence growing up. He said he saw violence while partying, at football, on the block, most everywhere he was. "It became normal to see violence," he said. "I even saw someone close to me shoot a person right in front of me." He said he saw people get shot more than once, and witnessed a man who was shot right next to him. He said he did not try to help the wounded man because "of the mentality I was pushing then." Renaldo said "I don't know he. I ain't helping he. He's not my family or no friend of mine."

He admitted that he was full of a lot of anger, but was unsure where it came from. He believed that information of a domestic nature was being withheld from him, and he was searching for things that he probably should not be searching for.

Renaldo also believed that he was not embraced by his older brothers. "They never showed me the way, whether right or wrong. I looked up to them, but they never embraced me," he said. He felt left out both by them and his friends from his community.

JAMAR BYNOE

Jamar Bynoe was born on June 17th, 1991 to Maxine and Julian. His father was occasionally off the island due to the latter's participation in the Canadian Farm Labour programme. Jamar's father eventually left him, migrating to Canada when Jamal was around the age of 4 years old.

During his upbringing, Jamar lived between his mother and his uncle. According to him, his uncle was more easygoing, "more free-up"; compared to his mother who was more restrictive with his movements.

He attended St Mary's Primary school, and later passed the 11 plus exam for Lester Vaughn School. According to Jamar, everyone was shocked that he passed for Lester Vaughn Secondary school because he was considered a slow learner. When he did pass for the school, he received a trophy from Patrick Todd, Member of Parliament for the area. "I couldn't read or count good," he said. However, he improved in Class 4 in primary school with his mother teaching him the tables in preparation for the Common Entrance Exam. Jamar navigated through Lester Vaughn School and eventually received 4 CXCs, all at Grades 3.

He would work at Young's supermarket on Saturdays from the age of 12 as a packer. He worked there for a year and was let go for coming to work late and taking long hours for lunch. Not too long after, he went to work at Less Frill super-market in a similar capacity.

Childhood deviance

When asked about his school days, Jamar said he used to get into a lot of trouble. "I was uncontrollable," he said. "I would run away for fun and adventure. My mother would go searching and get the whole community to look for me."

When he was around 8 years old, he remembers taking up his younger brother who was 5 years old at the time; and just left home for a couple of hours. "It was an adventure for me, I liked doing it." He also brought home a little girl from primary school one day under the premise that he was having a birthday party. The school was contacted and Jamar was recommended for counselling.

"I used to walk away for adventure," he said. Oftentimes, someone would find him and take him to the police station.

So concerned were his teachers and Principal at St Mary's Primary School, that by their recommendation, he was seen by a Psychologist from the Ministry of Education and the Child Care Board.

Jamar admitted to smoking cigarettes from Class 4 in Primary School and marijuana from the first form in secondary school.

He also indicated that he was also troublesome at secondary school. He was involved in many fights, gambled frequently, skipped classes and pulled off pranks. One prank he often did was calling in bomb threats "nuff times" so he could get to go home early or go to the beach or by a particular girlfriend. Another prank he admitted to doing was putting stones in his teacher's vehicle muffler.

He was sent to the Principal's office on many occasions and was flogged just as many. He admitted that one day, he wrote a letter to the Principal, and forged his mother's signature, saying not to beat him anymore, and the Principal stopped flogging him.

Jamar was also sent to the Juvenile Liaison Scheme (JLS). JLS is part of the Royal Barbados Police Force and serves to steer children who commit crimes or are prone toward deviant behaviours from the criminal justice system Jamar went to the Juvenile Liaison Scheme three times – one for fighting and twice for theft. He also admitted to stealing from stores in Bridgetown. At the time, he was in 3rd form at Lester Vaughn Secondary School.

He recalled that a male police officer at the Juvenile Liaison Scheme wanted to send him to Government Industrial School, Dodds. However, a female police officer said that he looked innocent and suggested he gets counselling instead.

Jamar said that he was selling marijuana from 4th form at Lester Vaughn school. "I also used to hustle from third form – bobbies, chewing gum, lollipops. I wanted money to gamble." He said that he did not want to ask his mother for money, especially on Saturdays.

He admitted that he got suspended in 4th form once for fighting at school. At the time, he was gambling, and lost all the money (bus fare, everything), so "I snatched up all the pool, so everyone was vex." He busted a fellow student's head with a piece of metal and the security guard at the school had to pull them apart. He and the student were taken to the Principal, Mr Ezra Carter who suspended them for two weeks. Jamar was sent to Edna Nicholls school, a school for children who exhibit troublesome or deviant behaviours, for a week.

Jamar said that in 3rd form, he wasn't focused. He blamed the dancehall and street culture for his lack of focus - "the reggae, bashment vans, hot girls" captured his attention. He said school work was dull and boring for him. However, his behavior captured the attention of his Food and Nutrition teacher, Miss Blades. She carried him through a very serious talk when she noticed the road he was taking.

"You are wasting your time," she said. "Some of these friends you are following, you will never see again after you leave school. You must look at your school work more seriously." Jamar reflected on his teacher's words and started to take his school work a little more seriously, and was signed up to take CXC exams. He tried very hard not to get into any conflicts, but as fate would have it, he got into another fight when he was 15 years old with a school mate whom he said started it. Jamar hit him with a pipe in his head.

He was hauled to the Principal who expelled him, but allowed him to come in just to sit his CXCs. Jamar strongly believes that if he was allowed to stay in school, that he would have done better in his CXCs since he had to study on his own without any guidance from school teachers.

Jamar blamed himself partially for his expulsion. It is worthy to mention that according to a later interview with Jamar's mother, she indicated that she was unaware that her son was indeed suspended.

Nevertheless, Jamar took home the expulsion paper, left it under a bowl and packed a bag and went straight to live with his uncle until his mother calmed down.

He started working at Jordan's supermarket after he had a talk with the owner of the supermarket, Mr. Jordan, and explained his circumstances to him. "I didn't want to be on the block," he said. He explained to Mr Jordan that he was doing CXCs and he got a job as a pack out boy while he did his CXCs.

After he started getting money, he started to live carefree. "I was a child, but still an adult," he said. He was living back and forth between his uncle and his mother. He started partying and living the wild life with the girls. However, he affirmed that he was a saver and spent the money he received in tips while saving his wages.

His mother and cousin wanted him to join the Barbados Youth Service. After much consideration, he chose to sign up. He stated that he totally enjoyed the experience, and would recommend any young person to join.

Love for cooking

Jamar had a love for food. He saw food as an art and was signed up to be in the Junior Chef competition but dropped out as he could not get along with his partner in the competition.

He enrolled at the Pomme Marine hotel for a year-long General Catering course and finished in 2009. He then held a few jobs afterwards; at Inland Revenue, handling income tax returns; and with his brother in his freighting business.

Red Rock Restaurant

Jamar got a job in November 2009 at Red Rock Restaurant in Dover, Christ Church as a Cook. He remembers that he loved the job but got too accustomed to the menu and he wanted a change. A girl that worked with him at Red Rock told him about an Australian restaurant named Ozzie's. She told him she was leaving to go there and tried to encourage him to go with her. According to Jamar, "I tried talking her out of it."

Shortly afterwards, he was offered a job there, but didn't want to leave "sure for unsure", as many restaurants opened up and closed in a short space of time in the area. However, he changed his mind and told his friend that he would work both jobs. He told the boss at Red Rock that he wanted to work only mornings because he wanted to work at Ozzie's at night.

He then went to work at Ozzie's but only worked there for 3 days because he didn't like the atmosphere. He then went back to his full time schedule at Red Rock restaurant.

Trouble at Red Rock restaurant

Jamar was sent home for a day after getting in to work late. According to him, he got to work 3 hours late and didn't call to say he was going to be late. This is Jamar's account of the events:

"After I was sent home for the day, someone called me later that day and told me that my supervisor (Kelly)'s car was burning. I was off the 9th of July. Her car burnt on the 8th of July 2010. Kelly called him on the job and asked him if he burnt her car. He told her no, he didn't burn her car. I worked for 2-3 days, got gastroenteritis on the Monday and was supposed to be off on the Wednesday.

I came in to work the next day and saw another chef on duty and was told to report to Kelly, who fired me from Red Rock for abandoning my job, even though I submitted a sick paper," said Jamar, but he was adamant she fired him because she believed he burnt her car.

Kelly worked at Red Rock restaurant and hired Jamar on the 19th November 2009. She was responsible for supervising him up to July 2010 when he was fired. However, she saw a change in Jamar after he turned 19. "He had two personalities. The guy I fired in July 2010 was not the Jamar I met at 18. It was the devil himself. The look on his face was an evil one, it was just not him, it was someone else," she stressed.

Kelly remembered Jamar as a pleasant person who showed great ambition initially. "I used to pick him up and take him to and from work sometimes," she recalled. However, Jamar started to get to work late and it became a problem. "One Thursday afternoon (8th July), I had to send him home for the day because he was coming in late constantly for about a month and that particular day, he turned up very late." She had spoken to him on several occasions. His excuses were not reasonable and did not sound truthful.

Torching his boss' car

"Later that day, my car was torched. I didn't even think at the time that it was Jamar, until the guys in restaurant told me they believed it was him. I will never forget the next day when Jamar came to work and I spoke to him on the phone. I asked Jamar if it was him who torched my car, and all he said very flatly and very softly was 'no, hold on', and handed another colleague on the phone. I cried when he did that because I knew then it was him," Kelly recalled.

Kelly stated that two molotov cocktails were found next to her car. "He also threw a rock in my car, which landed in my baby seat," she recalled. However, the Molotov cocktails did not land in the car. They were at the side. There were also matches, about an entire box of matches, which were emptied at the front and back of the car.

"I didn't know what was his intention," said Kelly. "I cried because this was the same car that took him to and from work."

Jamar then called out sick the Saturday and Sunday, and he was supposed to be off the Monday and Tuesday. He was scheduled to come to work on the Wednesday but he never came to work, and called in sick the Thursday and Friday too. Kelly then called his house and told the person on the other end of the phone to inform Jamar that he had to bring in sick certificate. The sick certificate came in on the Friday for another week or two. After the end of the certified period on the sick certificate, Jamar came back to work.

Kelly then explained how and why she dismissed Jamar.

"I fired Jamar because he absented himself from work. When he did turn up to work, I called him in and told him that unfortunately I was letting him go because he fired himself because he didn't come to work for three consecutive days. However, before I called him in, I took off the handle of the guillotine and sharpened it, because in my mind I was telling myself that if I sent him home for one day and he torched my car, what would he do to me now that I am firing him? I was scared of him. I had to prepare for the worst," said Kelly. "He had shaved off all the hair off his body – his head, his eyebrows, everything. I told myself that this can get ugly. He looked evil," she said.

"It was only after my car was torched, that I started learning more about Jamar. I learnt that he spray-painted the shoes of a guy at work due to a conflict between the two of them. I also learnt that he told one of the female employees, Margaret that he was going to poison her," said Kelly.

"One of the guys at work said to me that he (Jamar) was asking one of them how to get a gun and he sent him to another guy, who called him back and said "this guy does not want a gun – he wants C4 (explosives)!!" recalled Kelly.

"After the Chicken Galore firebombing occurred, and I heard about the method used, I called the police and spoke to the same police woman who handled the torching of my car. I told her I suspected that it was Jamar, because of what he did to my car, and because he lived close to where it happened, and her response was "let the police do their job," said Kelly.

After Kelly heard of the Campus Trendz tragedy, she said she went through phases of being scared and angry. She asked herself "how close could I have come to having Campus Trendz happen to me? What if I had gotten in the car and he threw the Molotov cocktail? What if he had targeted me like he targeted those girls?"

She also recalls Jamar being excited that he learnt how to make the smoke effect that is seen on stages and he told her that one day he will be famous, but she never paid attention to these proclamations.

Kelly said that as a result of what had happened to her, she no longer drives to work. "I leave my car at home," she said.

Red flags from home

Jamar's brother said in an interview that there were red flags surrounding his brother and his behavior, but they did not take them seriously. Jamar had no strange behaviours, but would watch a lot of Burn Notice (a television series) on cable. They however admitted that his behavior changed. "We were wondering if he was involved in a cult or some form of initiation into something. He would say some strange things sometimes.

After the Chicken Galore firebombing, his brother became suspicious about Jamar's involvement in the incident. He noticed burns on his feet that were oozing.

Jamar was using blackies off the block. His brother noticed that he could smell them on him when he came in the door Three of his siblings held on to him and beat him, and asked him if he was in a gang. According to his brother, Jamar just took the blows and said nothing. Jamar told them he got the burns from hot oil splashing on his feet. His brother then later believed that it was probably from gasoline spilling on his foot.

"My girlfriend said to me that the still picture taken in the Chicken Galore case looked like Jamar," he said. He started pondering on it, but tried to dismiss it as Jamar came home and went back to Chicken Galore with two other boys and came home with chicken.

After the Campus Trendz murders, his brother was on the computer and looking at the girls' images on the computer and saying "Chaa, these six beautiful girls gone and dead. Whoever do this, the police going to mash them up." His brother was next to him when he said this and said nothing nor displayed no emotion.

"Jamar continued in there like nothing happened every day until the police came and picked him up off the block," said his brother.

His brother feels he betrayed himself for not doing more about Jamar's behaviours.

"Jamar got a tattoo of a cemetery with 6 tombstones on his abdomen area with a psalm next to them. These tattoos were apparently done after the Campus Trendz incident," said his brother. It made him ponder how they could have missed the signs or if there was anything they could have done.

Conviction

Jamar was convicted for murder in 2016 in the Supreme Court of Barbados and sentenced to death for the Campus Trendz murders. Through his attorney-at-law, Andrew Pilgrim, SC, he appealed his conviction with the Court of Appeal in June 2022.

Pilgrim's argument was that it was inappropriate for the Director of Public Prosecutions to proceed with a murder charge against his client while it accepted a manslaughter plea from his co-accused, Renaldo Anderson Alleyne, who according to him, was the "primary actor" in the women's deaths.

The Court of Appeal denied his application and upheld his conviction in June 2022. However, the Court set aside his death sentence and ordered that he be resentenced by the High Court.

Jamar later took his appeal to the highest appeal court, the Caribbean Court of Justice, (CCJ). The CCJ also denied his application and his murder conviction remains.

CHICKEN GALORE ROBBERY AND FIREBOMBING

Renaldo stated that it was Jamar who first brought the idea to him about robbing an establishment and firebombing it. "Jamar got the idea from off the internet," said Renaldo. The purpose of the firebombing was to destroy evidence. Chicken Galore in Bank Hall, St Michael was targeted as the business to rob in this way.

Renaldo shared some of the chilling details of the Chicken Galore Robbery

On August 13th, 2010, both Renaldo and Jamar planned on robbing Chicken Galore. They entered the premises around 3:25 p.m. The cashier was serving a customer. Renaldo pretended to be a customer. Unmasked, Jamar placed a haversack on the counter and stuck up the cashier with a cutlass and demanded the money. The cashier panicked, gave him the money and dropped some of the cash. Jamar then took out a Molotov cocktail, lit it and threw it behind the counter where the cashier was standing. She ran and shortly after, everyone in the chicken depot ran outside. The entire establishment was burnt.

Jamar ran from Chicken Galore with the loot of $1,000.00. The two men then split the proceeds of the robbery equally. They used the money to buy "supplies for the drug world" – weed, wrappers, 'fantas' and cigarettes.

According to the court, the estimated damage to the building and stock was approximately $330,000.00.

According to Renaldo, the drug business was booming from the proceeds, but as it was only $500.00 he received, it didn't last too long.

As the Chicken Galore robbery was considered successful, they then planned on another robbery. Renaldo referred to the execution of the robbery as "getting off a set", a term apparently used on the street, where the plan is to get to the venue, commit the act and get out as quickly as possible.

CAMPUS TRENDZ ROBBERY AND FIREBOMBING

Campus Trendz was located on the ground floor of a two-storey wall constructed building at #48, Tudor Street, St Michael. There were no back doors to the building. The ground floor was separated from the first floor by a concrete floor. Two of the doors to the front served as the entry and exit to Campus Trendz boutique and the other served the same purpose for the first floor.

Campus Trendz offered clothing, shoes, bags and accessories. Their daily activities were captured and retained on a DVR recorder system. The boutique was opened to business that Friday from 10:00 a.m. to 8:00 p.m.

The boutique was staffed by four employees: Pearl Cornelius, Shanna Griffith, Kellishaw Ollivierre and Odessa Niles.

Approximately two days before the Campus Trendz tragedy, both Renaldo and Jamar went around the Campus Trendz store area and surveyed it. They looked at the layout. They chose Campus Trendz because it was a clothes store, and they figured money had to be in there. They said it had to be booming with people on Tudor Street and must have a good set of money. They checked for a getaway route. According to Renaldo, the route was one that would "swing back into town back next to a building that would put you at Hutson Alley".

The specific time was relevant. They didn't want it to be too early, and they wanted it to be a time to pick up sales. They then decided that 5:00 p.m. was a good time.

On September 3rd, 2010, the two men decided to carry out the robbery. Outside was still bright. They left home and headed to the store. Renaldo recounted "When I was about to walk in the store, Jamar told me to walk past the store. I ask myself why he telling me to walk past the store. I obeyed and we passed all the people liming. I walked straight down to KFC. There were not a lot of people near the store. We stopped and I asked him what happen that he made me walk past the store. He said he wanted to scope the scene. He asked me "you ready?"

Renaldo further recounted, "I then had a thought, call this off, this already fail. I tell he yes, I ready, let we go along. I told him I will go through the top door. I was ahead of him. When I get right by the door, I had a mask and put it on in the store. I had an adrenaline rush. My mission was to get in and get out. He swing through the other door. No one was paying us any mind. All when we were in the store, no one outside knew what was going on. I had a small knife. No one was supposed to come out until we allowed them to come out."

There were about seven customers in the store, including Kelly Ann Welch, Nikkita Belgrave and Tiffany Harding.

The owner was sitting near the area of the cash register, while her daughter was standing backing the door of the store. The salesgirls were assisting customers.

Renaldo and Jamar, armed with knives and with Renaldo wearing the mask, entered the store. Renaldo recounts: "An old lady and a fellow were on my right. The old lady paused. The guy was trying to get past me. I stopped him. I had the two Molotov cocktails. They were made from glass bottle with gasoline and a piece of rag pushed in the Banks bottle. The rag was soaked in gasoline. If lit, it will catch. If the bottle drops and breaks, it will spread." However, according to Renaldo, "I didn't see the need for the cocktails, because whoever see me has to respect us as robbers when they see us with the knives."

Meanwhile, Odessa, one of the sales clerks at Campus Trendz was assisting three customers. One of these customers was looking for a pair of shoes for herself for about 20 minutes. Her cell phone rang and she turned away to answer. When she answered the cellphone and turned around to face the door, she saw a man with a green mask from army material around his face. She thought it was a prank. Odessa shouted that someone was robbing the store and ran towards the back of the store. There, the three customers ran behind Odessa in a room at the back, which was later discovered to be the storeroom.

Three other girls, who were employees of the store ran into the bathroom further into the rear of the store.

Renaldo stated that he was unaware that persons ran to the back of the store. His focus was on the front. "Jamar was around by the cash register, waiting. The cash register was short there by the left hand side. He had a lady hold up, who I later learnt was the owner of the store. She put up a resistance. He gave her a stab in her foot. After he stabbed her in her left thigh, I started to get a little impatient 'cos nothing was happening. I moved and went to the cashier."

It was during this time that Renaldo lit one of the two bottles filled with gasoline and threw it to the rear section of the store, setting the clothes on fire.

Jamar continued to pull the owner to the cash register where he told her to open it and in her failed attempts, tried opening it himself. Having not being able to get the cash register opened, the owner's daughter seeing what happened, shouted to her mother and told her what to press to get the register opened. The owner complied and the cash register opened. At this point, Renaldo had joined Jamar in his attempt to open the cash register.

After it opened, the two took the money from the cash pan and placed it in their pockets. By this time, the entire store was engulfed in flames.

Renaldo stated: "I doubt we were in the store for a minute. I opened one of the bottles and lit it and toss it out of my hand, then went to the cash register and started to bang on it and get all the money I could with my hand and stuffed it in the bag on the cash register. I told him it's time to go. I then lit the other cocktail. On my exit, I threw the second one because I had no other use for it."

Patrons and staff screamed and ran in different directions. According to the judgement in Renaldo's appeal, the six females concealed themselves in the bathroom and storeroom towards the rear of the building, not knowing that the conflagration was about to overwhelm the entire store. An alarm was raised, and the Fire Department and Police arrived and took control of the scene. Screams were heard coming from the bathroom and the storeroom. These screams continued for a while.

Daniel Niles, who was hanging around liming on the outside, rushed into the burning store and tried to put out the fire, but was unsuccessful. Determined to put out the blaze, Niles ran to the business *Urban Beauty Supplies*, located a few stores down and borrowed a fire extinguisher. He returned to Campus Trendz, but found the heat too intense to enter. He then stood on the sidewalk and sprayed the contents of the fire extinguisher into the store.

Neville Todd, owner of Urban Beauty which was a few doors away from Campus Trendz, saw the building on fire, and witnessed the men running away, and was able to see that one of the men was in a crouching position with his head down. Todd ran in and shut his door, since he suspected something sinister was happening. He heard an explosion, and the store owner ran to him and said "Mr Todd, help, help! They just rob the place, and burn it!" He looked out and saw smoke coming from the store.

Renaldo and Jamar ran along Tudor Street towards the Milk Market, and turned left onto an opened lot beside Urban Beauty Supplies into Hutson Alley. "As soon as I got through the alley, I took off my mask," said Renaldo.

He stated that Jamar was ahead of him, leading the way because he knew the escape route better than him. However, according to Renaldo "he got to a part that got me angry. We were on a getaway spree and Jamar stopped on a block in Hutson Alley to shout a cousin. I asked him 'what you doing?' and he left." This, according to the reports, is where they were seen by several men who were liming. Two of the men recognised Jamar from attending primary school with them.

The Campus Trendz fire

Meanwhile back in Tudor Street, one of the shoppers who ran into the store room, peeped through a space under the door and recognised the building was on fire. She informed the others that the store was burning and suggested that they all leave the room. The others in the room pleaded with her not to go outside, since they were of the opinion that the assailants were still there. She insisted and opened the store-room door. At this point, the flames were not too high and she ran out of the store followed by the other persons in the room with her.

As the fire intensified, screams were heard coming from the bathroom where the other ladies had concealed themselves. Attempts were made to rescue the girls from the burning building but without success. The girls were texting their loved ones constantly pleading for help, then their texts stopped, and their screams and cries went silent.

The Fire Department fought valiantly to gain access to the building which by then was engulfed in flames. The fire and the heat were too much. The firemen resorted to breaking a wall at the back of the building to gain access to the bathroom and the storeroom. By then it was too late for the trapped females. The six young women were found huddled together dead.

Meanwhile, the two perpetrators continued their getaway from the scene of the crime. "We ended out by the road by the Cheapside Post Office. We were walking and saw two patrol policemen. The closer we got, I started talking to make it look like we late for the bus. It appeared as though they (the police) noticed that something was up in Baxters Road as they were looking in that direction."

"We got in a van that put us out by Vietnam (a block) by Westbury Cemetery. We went through the gap. On going through the gap, I started taking off the clothes and threw them in the garbage out by Vietnam. Jamar started doing the same thing too. We went in to St Leonard's cemetery and picked up clothes in a haversack that was stashed before we did the deed. We collected it and changed and walked up the road, and went home."

"I went home, bathed and counted the money and split it up," Renaldo said. He does not remember how much it was, but it was not much money. "I went back on the block breezing. A couple hours later, we heard that six girls were trapped in the store. My reaction was like 'what the hell? How this happened?' We weren't looking for other people to be in there."

Meanwhile, Jamar disposed of the shades, clothing and bag he wore by placing them in a garbage can by his uncle's home. He threw the knife he used in St Leonard's church yard.

Renaldo recalled "I then heard the fellows on the block talking. One fellow said he could see smoke somewhere burning. I kept quiet and said nothing. One of the other fellows said "they like they had a big robbery in Baxters Road. I decided to stop on the block with the fellows."

"I felt totally horrible. It had me offset. I wasn't looking for nobody to be in there. I decided to just stay cool. I went karaoke that same night in Greenfield, St Michael."

"The next day, September 4th, I heard that the six girls that were trapped in the store passed away. It erupted another set of emotions with me," said Renaldo. "I didn't want to go around people. I started to withdraw more. I asked the shopkeeper to see the paper and follow the story. The shopkeeper was hysterical. He said that the person want locking up. The shopkeeper didn't know that the person was standing right next to him."

"Jamar was scared. I took a walk with him and asked him how he felt. I didn't want to talk to him. I told him let's just go about the day like normal."

"Then the police leads started coming out. The first lead was a sketch. It looked just like Jamar," said Renaldo. However, according to him, Jamar   denied it looked like him.

Police artist sketch of one of the murderers

The second lead was the Chicken Galore CCTV. Footage from the firebombing showed an image of Jamar, which according to Renaldo, easily identified him.

The tragedy was on his mind every single day. Jamar was constantly in denial. Renaldo stated that the duo agreed that Jamar was supposed to be on the down low as no one saw his (Renaldo's) face. "I can walk about because nobody didn't see my face," said Renaldo.

"The next Friday, September 10th, 2010, I saw Jamar sitting on a block. I said to him, 'why are you sitting on the block?' I started to get paranoid. I rolled a spliff while I was on the block and had headphones in my ear. I pretended to be listening to the music but I had one mic in and the other out to hear what was going on and what people were talking about."

Busted!

"Out of the corner of my eye, I got a glance at a man in a COW Williams construction company uniform. He had a gas can in his hand, and stopped by the opening in the block. He put down the gas can. On his way up in a standing position, I saw the man draw a firearm and put it on Jamar. He said 'we come for you!' I looked to the right and saw undressed police. Two were coming through the canal, and two were coming through the gate of the canal. On their way coming up, I was going out. I didn't go home. I called a fellow on the block to find out what was going on. He said 'nuff police out here. They got Jamar I told him if something happen, let me know."

"I continued playing the game of not knowing what was going on. I stayed outside until 3 a.m. I left, went home and couldn't sleep that night. I slept for a half hour. I got up, bathed, changed clothes, and went outside about 4:30 a.m. I went back in the area until the sun came up. The men started coming outside. Nobody discussed what happened last night. It was a new day.

"I took a little stroll and went by my girlfriend. She is a very observant person and she could tell something was bothering me. She kept asking me what was wrong but I said nothing. I then got a text message saying that 'the police got my man Jamar and that they have him questioning for the scene that happened in Baxters Road'."

"My objective was to leave there, go home, get the necessary things and disappear. No communication whatsoever. I didn't know where I was going to go.

"I left by my girlfriend and got stick up on the block name *Roachville*. I went home and had on my pants and socks. The phone rang. My sister said the phone was for me. For me? Nobody don't call me on the house phone! A woman was on the phone asking me why I didn't meet her in Tudor Street. I kept asking the woman who she is and she won't say but kept repeating the question. I then hung up the phone on the person."

"As soon as I hung up, about seven to eight police officers came through the front door with guns and grabbed me! They said we are carrying you in the bedroom. They skinned up my entire bedroom. They told me to put on your shoes and shirt, handcuffed me and carried me outside. I saw all the neighbourhood outside." That was the last time he saw his neighbourhood.

"The police then took me to Major Crimes Unit in the Glebe in St George and I gave a statement about the Campus Trendz tragedy, as they showed me a statement where my name was used as being linked to the tragedy. I was in custody for three days until I was charged with six counts of murder related to the Campus Trendz robbery."

When asked whether they had intended to do a similar crime in the future if this robbery was successful, Renaldo said yes, but this time with no firebombs. He would have escalated it to guns instead of bombs.

Remorse

Renaldo expressed remorse for his crimes. He said he genuinely did not know that other people were in the store. "When you stop in the store, you do not know other people were in the store. It looked deserted". In his words, Renaldo said "it was just a robbery that went bad".

He penned a letter to the family of the victims dated January 23rd, 2017 which partly reads as follows:

"To the families, friends and associates of the Campus Trendz Disaster: Victims:

This is the hardest letter I have ever had to write but I want you to hear the truth. I am in prison because I broke the law. It is entirely my own fault, and now I must pay a heavy penalty.

It is hard being a man and facing the truth... because I have learnt that when you make a mistake, you are the only one who can truly correct it, it is totally up to you to do everything that you can to undo any harm or pain you may have caused... and the sincere truth is that I can neither undo my actions nor stop the pain that I have caused the family and friends of the six young ladies.

I am so, so sorry...and these words are sincerely spoken from my heart. I am sorry for all the pain, heartache, loss, confusion and despair my actions would have and is still causing to all of you. How could I ever hope to ameliorate this with mere words? Gawd, I am so sorry.

I am asking now... no!... I am begging each and every one of you, to find a small space within your hearts to forgive me. I also have a need – a desperate need to let you know that what happened was not intentional. I never meant to hurt anyone... I never in my life imagined things to get out of hand.

I was wrong for robbing Campus Trendz, my actions were malicious and reckless. I was at a selfish age... I only felt endlessly powerful and endlessly optimistic; my pockets were empty but my head was full of wild things. Sounds scary to me now even as I write... felt wonderful then... felt very cool.

Then my troubles set in. I never went to hurt anyone, all I wanted to do was get away. I never foreseen (sic) that people would have been trapped or the building would have caught so easily. I made a decision that changed so much and affected so much people... including me, and that decision took the innocent lives of six young ladies who had hopes, dreams and aspirations.

I have prayed and asked God to help us all. I know I can't relate to your grief, pain and troubles, because all I have done is taken...but I need you to understand that my pain, my sadness, my anguish, and my horrors is all because I have taken.

This whole situation has even changed the way I walk, the way I think about myself, and towards others...each and every day for the rest of my life, I will be thinking of what I did... I will be envisaging these young ladies over and over again in my dreams... I will always be thinking of *their children, their mothers and fathers, their brothers and sisters and loved ones... And I will always be saying to myself that I have taken what I or no one can ever replace and I have disrupted so many other lives at the same time.*

When I first came to prison, I was somewhat stuck (mentally and emotionally, if not physically). Then the years slid by and one day I found myself looking into the mirror with real puzzlement; that day I instantly prayed to God, asking him to touch the hearts and the lives of the families of these six young ladies, that they will forgive me.

Today I ask your forgiveness... I am reaching out to you, trying to let you understand what happened, and for forgiveness.

Please... to the families, friends, associates, and to all of Barbados... I am honestly and sincerely sorry.

Pained and Remorseful,

Always,

Renaldo Alleyne"

Sentence and Appeal

Renaldo Alleyne was charged with six counts of murder. On arraignment on June 1st, 2011, he pleaded not guilty to murder but guilty to six counts of manslaughter. These pleas were accepted by the then Director of Public Prosecution, the late Mr Charles Leacock QC. On August 15th, 2012, the trial judge, Her Ladyship Madame Justice Elneth Kentish, sentenced Renaldo Alleyne to six concurrent life sentences.

Renaldo appealed his conviction and the appeal of his sentence was heard on the 9th and 16th of November, 2016. He raised two grounds of appeal namely that: (i) the sentence of life imprisonment on each count was wrong in law and in principle in that the trial judge had failed to follow established guidelines in arriving at a sentence of life imprisonment and further that the sentences were excessive; and (ii) that the trial judge had disregarded and had failed to factor into the sentence the Appellant's entitlement to a discount for his guilty plea.

On October 4th, 2017, the Court of Appeal dismissed the appeal and affirmed the life sentences. The court held that the life sentences were neither wrong in principle, manifestly excessive nor disproportionate. The court also decided that while the general principle is that a discount can be given on a determinate sentence in the face of an early guilty plea, a discount is incompatible with an indeterminate sentence, such as a life sentence.

The Judge, in considering the appropriate sentence to be imposed upon the Appellant, reviewed agreed to facts and the self-written statement of the Appellant given to the police on September 11th, 2010. Renaldo's statement was as follows:

"Two Thursdays ago Jamar Bynoe came to me and said that he got this little mission to go on. He tell me that we going to rob this little clothes store on Reed Street. He didn't say the name of the store. I tell he that I would go with he. He tell me that he going to get back to me. The next day me and Jamar was just sitting down together down Headley Land breezing. Approximately around 6:00 p.m. we leave and went down in the gully in Headley's land. and collect a black haversack and walk and went through the Garden Land down Passage Road and went in St. Leonard's cemetery. Me and Jamar change off we clothes in the cemetery. I put on a blue long jean pants and a white long sleeve tee shirt. Jamar put on a black long pants and a greenish dress shirt. We leave our clothes in the cemetery to come back for them. We leave and went through a track that take us back out to Baxters Road and we walk straight down Baxters Road and when we got down Tudor Street Jamar nod his head to signal that that was the store. When we got down by KFC he gave me a plastic bag with two Banks beer bottles with something that smell like gasoline. The bottles had cloth stuff at the top. Jamar asked me if I frightened and I said 'yes'. We walk and come back down and he tell me that when we get by the store to walk straight in. He get into the store before me. He went in one door and I went through the next. I just heard screaming even before I put on my mask. I just put on my mask and walk in. He was there asking a lady to give us the money, and she resisted. I still had the plastic bag in my hand. I put down the bag tore it open and pull out one of the bottles. I say you taking so long, you ain't get through yet? I use a lighter I had in my pocket and I light one of the cocktails and tossed it in the store. I see Jamar struggling with a girl with the cash register. So I just went back with the other cocktail and she tried to open the cash register. I went and start hitting the cash register telling the girl to open it. She open the cash register and I stuck in my hand and grab the money I could get hold in my hand. I light the other cocktail and just [throw] it there right by the door. We ran out and ran through the first track side of the store. We ran through the track that lead to the Dog Pound. I kinda like run past where Jamar turn and he call me back and tell me I was going the wrong way. The tracks that we went through lead us back out by the Post Office. We decided to go and get in a van. The van took us around Harbour Road up the road by Kensington Oval and we got off by a bus stop. We went through a gap on the other side of the road and I [throw] my shirt in a blue garbage can. We went back in the cemetery and change off. We come back out through another track from the cemetery which leads to the road by Brydens. We went through a housing area and this lead up

back to Passage Road. We walk through the Garden Land I went home and bathe and change my clothes. Later the same night I meet Jamar in the yard of Hindsbury Primary School and we count up the money that we got from the store. It was about $1,200.00. I get $600.00 and he get $600.00. About six hours later, I hear people saying that Campus Trendz burn down and six people trap in it. I feel real sorry about this situation."

A psychological report dated July 8th, 2012, was prepared by Mr Sean Pilgrim, Psychologist at Her Majesty's Prisons, Dodds. The report alluded to Renaldo's unpleasant and difficult life which was plagued by a tumultuous relationship between his parents. He encountered difficulties at school and with his academics, and began his daily smoking of marijuana from age ten. The psychologist reported that Renaldo expressed deep regret and that he appeared sincerely remorseful for his actions which resulted in the six deaths at the clothing boutique. He indicated that he did not plan to start the fire and was surprised at how rapidly the events unfolded. He was willing to face the consequences for his actions but hoped the judge would be lenient and that the victims' families would forgive him. The Psychologist further reported that Renaldo's personality style involved a degree of adventurousness, risk-taking, and a tendency to be rather impulsive. Renaldo also scored very high on the Behavioural Coping and Personal Superstitious Thinking Scales (PSTS) which explored the degree to which individuals hold private superstitions directly associated with cynicism, feelings of helplessness and depression. However, the psychologist's report indicated that Renaldo did not directly suffer from any major psychological disturbances.

The Appellant Judge commenced her sentencing remarks by alluding to the fact that under Section 6 of the Offences Against the Person Act, the maximum sentence for manslaughter was life imprisonment and that the offences to which Renaldo had pleaded guilty were all violent offences as defined by the Penal System Reform Act. The judge then adverted to provisions in Sections 35 to 41 of the Penal System Reform Act as required when a custodial sentence was being contemplated. Specific reference was made to the requirement in Section 36 that the length of the sentence should be commensurate with the gravity of the offence and in furtherance of that mandate the judge considered the aggravating and mitigating factors.

In having regard to the aggravating factors, the judge considered that the gravity of the offence could not be over-emphasised. She referenced (1) the unlawful taking of six young lives in 'one fell swoop'; (2) the deliberate intention to rob armed with two Molotov cocktails; (3) the plan to change clothes before and after execution of the robbery; (4) the lack of thought and concern as to the horrendous consequences of throwing two highly combustible missiles into a clothing store in which there was a large number of shoppers; (5) the readiness to participate in the scheme to effect the egregious robbery; (6) the reckless, callous and indifferent manner in which the robbery was executed; and (7) the painful and horrible death of the six young women.

The judge found that the mitigating factors were Renaldo's early guilty plea, his clean record, his cooperation with the police during the investigation of the incident and the fact that he was only 20 years of age at the time of the commission of the offence. The judge next considered the pre-sentencing and psychological reports, both of which were in similar terms, noting Renaldo's traumatic childhood and the negative impact of drug use on many aspects of his life. The prevailing consideration weighing on the judge's mind seemed to be that Renaldo constituted a threat to the public's safety. She commented: "Of significance in the Psychological Report, is a concern expressed by Mr Pilgrim on your scores on the Behavioural Coping and Personal Superstitious Thinking Scales which suggest that you do not usually consider challenges in a manner which allows you to resolve problems effectively and it relates clearly to the level of thoughtlessness that you exhibited in the planning of this crime, because I do not accept that not for a moment did it ever cross your mind that those people would die that tragic death, but the problem is why did it not cross your mind and therein lies your danger to this society. The Psychological Report identifies an automatism that has allowed you to speculate on your life following incarceration even though you are aware of the likelihood of a substantial custodial sentence. That optimism, opines Mr Pilgrim, reveals that a degree of simple mindedness which was likely to feature heavily in your decision-making process, and it is that simple mindedness which have earlier described, has a frightening aspect of your character. And Mr. Pilgrim also opines that though it is not immediately obvious you are experiencing significant emotional and psychological problems which have affected your personality development and interpersonal relationships."

The judge was of the view that the mitigating factors did not in any way neutralise the gravity of the offences and that neither the circumstances of the offence nor the Appellant's circumstances as offender counterbalanced the aggravating factors. Having regard to those factors, the seriousness of the offences, the reprehensible conduct of Renaldo and specifically his major character flaw in being easily led, and the horrendous and chilling circumstances in which the young women met their untimely and wholly unwarranted deaths, the judge concluded that the appellant represented such a grave danger to the society that only a life sentence would be "commensurate with the seriousness of the offences and adequate to protect the public from serious harm" from him. The judge sentenced Renaldo to imprisonment for six concurrent life sentences and ruled that it was a condition of the sentence that during the period of incarceration, Renaldo be included in any treatment programmes that would address his cognitive deficiencies identified in the psychological report.

Renaldo further appealed his sentence to the Caribbean Court of Justice (CCJ) in 2018. The CCJ ruled that the aggravating and mitigating factors were identified and discussed by the judge and by the Court of Appeal. They ruled that "taking those factors into account and in order to secure the sentencing objectives evident in the sentencing remarks by the judge, whilst not ruling out the possibility of rehabilitation, it appears necessary that a recommendation be made for the minimum period of incarceration. We therefore recommend that a minimum period of incarceration for twenty-five (25) years is necessary to satisfy for the objectives of punishment and deterrence." In other words, Renaldo must spend at least 25 years in prison before consideration for release. The possibility exists that Renaldo, with good behaviour, could be released into society in his 40s.

THE VICTIMS

The CCJ conceded that they knew very little about the victims. However, according to their decision, "What we do know is that they were all innocent women who fell victim to Alleyne's dreadful acts. They had huddled together in the back of the store where they had concealed themselves, seeking protection from Alleyne and his criminal accomplice. As they succumbed to the noxious flames, their gut-wrenching screams, before they died, could be heard by those powerless to save them. When rescuers reached them, it was thought that Shanna Griffith could be saved. She was rushed to the hospital but, unfortunately, she was pronounced dead on arrival. None of these women deserved this cruel fate. Their respective families and loved ones must now forever bear the deep anguish of living with a huge void; a gaping hole that not even time will ever fully close. The grief of the bereaved was not just shared. It was multiplied. As the trial judge rightly noted, 'the whole society was shocked and traumatised by this experience'.

Tiffany Harding was born on February 20th, 1987 in the United States of America. She attended St Paul's Primary School and Alleyne Secondary School. She attained seven certificates at CXC. She went on to do additional evening studies at Springer Memorial School. She intended to have a career in nursing and had applied for admission to the Barbados Community College's nursing programme. She was a shopper at Campus Trendz. She was 23 years old and had no children.

Kelly-Ann Welch was born on November 6th, 1985. She attended Christ Church Girls' School and Deighton Griffith Secondary School. She had one brother. She was a member of the cadet corps at school and was very much a "fashionista". After graduating from secondary school, she worked at Annetta's Fashions, GC Services and NCO Financial Services. Kelly-Ann was a shopper at Campus Trendz. She was 24 years old and the mother of one child, Khalia.

Kellishaw Ollivierre was born on December 12th, 1985, in St Vincent. She attended the CW Prescod Primary School and the Intermediate High School. She attained GCE and CXC Certificates in Food and Nutrition, Home Management, Social Studies, Mathematics and Principles of English and Business. She migrated to Barbados where she completed courses in cosmetology. Kellishaw dreamt of owning her own beauty store. She resided with her aunt. Kellishaw found employment at Campus Trendz since it opened. She was 24 years old.

Nikkita Belgrave was born on December 23rd, 1986. She attended St Andrew's Primary, Alleyne School and Samuel Jackman Prescod Polytechnic where she successfully pursued studies in aesthetics. She was employed at the hairdressing salon known as "Hair 4 U" and had ambitions to become a professional aesthetician. Nikkita was a shopper at Campus Trendz. She was 23 years old and had no children.

Pearl Amanda Cornelius was born on November 12th, 1991 in Guyana. She attended Wilford Garden Primary in Guyana and came to Barbados at the age of ten years old. She attended the Deighton Griffith Secondary in Barbados where she attained six CXC certificates. Upon leaving secondary school, she did evening classes at Springer Memorial and had ambitions on becoming an accountant. Pearl was employed part-time as a store clerk at Campus Trendz for four years. She was 18 years old.

Shanna Griffith was born on November 18th, 1991. She attended Deacons Primary School and St James Secondary School. Her ambition was to become a chef in the hospitality industry. As a result, she worked part time in a hotel and had applied for admission to the Barbados Community College's hospitality programme. She resided with her parents. Shanna was employed at Campus Trendz for one month. She was 18 years old, and had no children.

Effects on those left behind

Odessa Niles, who was 27 years old at the time, worked a couple weekends in Campus Trendz. She was one of the persons who ran into the storeroom. She lives every day asking herself if she had run back into the store, what could have gone differently. She is now afraid of the dark. "If the electricity is off, I'm scared," she said. She said she is scared of people, especially people who wear scarves on their faces.

"When it comes to evenings, I panic. I do not like to walk through Tudor Street, but if the bus puts me off up there, I just give a slight side eye (of where the store was) and walk away," she softly said.

Every time she sees the girls' faces, she cries. She doesn't talk about it.

However, she reads her Bible and prays a lot to help her to deal with the ordeal that she has to relive constantly. She also has a strong family support system. Even with the support system, she says is it still hell. Sometimes, she just dreams. In one of her dreams, she saw Kellishaw. Kellishaw told her "I am good."

"I always gave them good advice. I talked to them about relationships. I was older than them," said Odessa.

Recalling the day that changed her life forever, she said after she ran out of the storeroom, she just sat on the road staring at the fire. "A lady told me get up and go home because you don't know if they are looking on to see if they can come back for you."

Odessa states, "I feel sorry for my friends. They didn't get a life nor a chance. I live every day wondering what I could have done to save them. Could I have hollered a little harder and they would have heard me?"

She said she did not attend any of the funerals. She could not bear to. She just wants to remember them alive.

As for the perpetrators, she said "I don't know their names. I refused to look at them or read the paper when they caught them." When it came to their remorse, she had these words to say: "I don't want no sorry from them. They aren't sorry, only sorry they got caught. I pray they never come out."

CHAPTER FIFTEEN
Conclusion/ Appendices

DISCUSSION

Violence, particularly homicides has reached a pandemic proportion world-wide. From statistics gathered throughout the region, and even internationally, it would appear that humans are becoming more violent, disputes are becoming more lethal, and the illegal use of firearms is at a crisis stage.

The Caribbean has not escaped this scourge and grapples with high homicide rates annually, particularly in the last 10-15 years. According to the International Journal of Emergency Mental Health and Human Resilience, countries such as Jamaica, Mexico, Trinidad and Tobago, Honduras, Nicaragua, Colombia, Puerto Rico, Brazil, and El Salvador are among those nations with the highest rates of homicide in the world (Boxill et al., 2007; Blake, 2002; Krug et al., 2002).

The effects of murders are deleterious to families, communities and the wider society. They evoke immeasurable physical, emotional and psychological damage which can go on for years after the event.

Typology and factors associated with murders

But what drives persons to take the life of another person, especially in some of the horrific ways which have been displayed in this book? As we have seen, there were different circumstances surrounding each of these murders. There are a wide range of motives (and for some there were no known motives) that compel people to injure or kill others. Robbery, revenge, rape and even mental illness such as psychopathy are all factors and motives to murder.

Before we go on to look at various typologies of homicide, it is important to acknowledge that there are contributing factors to violence and specifically, murder. An individual's biological makeup where s/he has low intelligence, brain damage, a history of abuse, is suffering from psychosis, substance abuse and lack of social bonds to social institutions, are all contributing factors to placing that person at risk of engaging in violent behaviours. There are also community contexts, such as neighbourhoods or communities where violence is culturally accepted. In such cases, the community suffers from social isolation/exclusion and there is nothing that binds the community together. These factors are all important in understanding the context of criminality among persons who engage in crime and at-risk behaviour.

Researchers have developed homicide typologies to profile and explain the personality and motivations of homicide offenders.

One such typology is between organised and disorganised offenders. With the organised offender, the key is their planning of crime. Their crimes are planned, not spontaneous or spur of the moment. According to research, their planning derives from their fantasies, which develop over time.

Most victims of organised offenders are targeted strangers (such as the canefield murders). The offender stakes out or patrols an area, hunting for someone who fits a certain type of victims (age, appearance, occupation, lifestyle, gender).

The organised offender often uses a ruse or con to gain control over his victims. He tends to have good verbal skills and a high degree of intelligence, enough to lure a victim into a vulnerable area. Control is the essence for an organized offender. Because the crime has been planned, the offender has devoted time to figuring out how to obtain a victim and may have perfected the ruse.

Further evidence of planning that sometimes becomes available to police investigations lies in the organized offender's use of restraints – handcuffs, ropes and the like. Similarly, they bring their own weapon to the crime and take it away when they are finished. Sometimes, they take personal items that belong to their victims as trophies or to deny the police the possibility of identifying the victim.

The truly organised offender generally completes a sexual act with a living victim, taking full advantage of the situation to rape and torture before murdering someone.

They take steps to hide the bodies of their victims or otherwise attempt to conceal their identity, and then keep track of the investigation.

The actions of disorganized offenders however, are devoid of logic. Generally, no one can follow their reasoning for their actions. The disorganized offender does not care about fingerprints or other evidence.

Mental illness

One of the contributing factors to homicide is mental illness. In the book, there is clear evidence of mental illness in some of these cases, even as mentioned above regarding the serial killer and the canefield murders.

There is a link between mental disorder and crime. Research points to the fact that levels of mental disorders among prisoners tend to be higher than in the general population. However, the research states that it is not clear whether their mental disorder is related to their crimes or developed in prison. Only a minority of mentally disordered people offend, but many offenders have a mental disorder. People with schizophrenia for instance, are generally found to be at a higher risk for violence when compared to the wider population, and this risk increases with concomitant substance abuse (see Wallace et al, 2004).

Psychopathy is directly linked to violence and criminal behaviour. Psychopathic offending can be viewed as the result of the basic features of the disorder, e.g. callousness, impulsivity, egocentricity, grandiosity, irresponsibility, lack of empathy, guilt or remorse (Hare, 2003). Compared to other offenders, psychopaths begin offending at an earlier age, commit a wider variety of crimes, pose serious management problems while incarcerated and violate parole and/or re-offend sooner once released (Hare, 2003).

The relationship between psychopathy and violence is particularly important as psychopathic violence appears more dispassionate and predatory. Further, psychopathic violence appears motivated by factors such as greed, vengeance, anger, retribution or personal gain, and is mostly directed against strangers (Hare, 1999). Also, sexual homicides committed by psychopaths have been found to be more gratuitous and sadistic, with victims tending to be strangers (Porter et al, 2003). Psychopathic offending, however, does not result from a deluded mind, but as Hare states "from a cold, calculating rationality combined with a chilling inability to treat others as thinking, feeling human beings' (1993:5).

Robbery

As it relates to robberies, some robberies stem most directly from a perceived need for quick cash, but due to the prevailing street culture for which many robbers are directly a part of, many of these offenders are caught up in a cycle of expensive, self-indulgent habits (gambling, drug use, drinking) that feed on themselves and call for more of the same– in other words, the cycle continues. They rob, as in the case of Campus Trendz robbery and murder, to engage in habits such as buying marijuana, partying and gambling which in itself calls for more money and the act of robbery must be repeated.

The street culture values the pleasure seeking pursuit of stimulating the senses, of spontaneity, and denial of individual responsibility. The street culture typifies the need to constantly prove that one is hip, cool, and "in" by conspicuous displays and outlays of cash. Generally, robbers who are successful tend not to use their ill-gotten gains to anything of substance, but to live in the now, and live the wild carefree life. Naturally, such behaviours create the very reinforcing conditions that drive offenders to rob in the first place, but according to the research, such financial motivations usually become more a matter of maintaining a certain lifestyle and self-image. In other words, few robbers rob to really support a family.

Groth (1979) believed that rapists were more likely to express their need for power through rape and hostility. He developed a typology that emphasized the sexual act of rape as a way in which to express inner aggression and the need to control.

The Massachusetts Treatment Centre Taxonomic Programme (MTCTP) in the USA tested earlier motivational typologies and developed later models. The MTC:R3 classifies rapists based on the four primary motivations of Opportunistic, Pervasive Anger, Sexual and Vindictiveness.

Those within the Opportunistic category were impulsive and predatory. The Pervasive Anger category described those who were primarily motivated by highly generalised aggressive feelings. The Sexual category was thought to include those who were either sadistic (driven by a fusion of sexual urges and aggression) or non-sadistic (enthused by feelings of sexual inadequacy and the need to dominate).

Serial killers

As it relates to the canefield murders, Barbados was faced with a serial killer in the 1980s. The Federal Bureau of Investigations (FBI) categorises a serial killer as "a person who must first complete three separate murders that are spaced by a duration which they call "the cooling off period" which can vary from a few days to years."

Most serial killers in the United States are white males in their 20s or 30s, who target strangers near their homes or work places. In terms of choosing their victims, 62% of the killers target strangers exclusively and another 22% kill at least one stranger. In addition, 71% operate in a specific location or area, rather than travelling long distances to commit their crimes.

A local psychologist, interviewed by Carol Martindale at the **Nation** newspaper, iterated that it was necessary to delve into the background of murderers, especially one deemed a serial killer to see what makes him or her function.

And they recommended that this background search starts from the adolescent years. "Most serial killers come from dysfunctional backgrounds involving sexual or physical abuse, drugs or alcoholism," he said.

It is also believed that a number of serial killers might have been avoided if the killers were treated better in their younger days.

The impact of homicides on those left behind

When someone is murdered, the death is sudden, violent, final and senseless. The surviving family or co-victims are left to come to grips with the reality that their loved one, friend, neighbour, is no longer there.

Survivors of homicide victims, also called co-victims, are generally defined as the family members, friends, and other loved ones of the victim. They too are victims in their own right. The violent, unexpected death of their loved one is one of the most traumatic experiences they will probably ever face, and it usually prompts a wide range of emotional reactions. Indeed, the psychological issues co-victims have to contend with are more serious than the problems victims of other kinds of crimes experience (Lamet and Wittebrood, 2009; Rando, 1996; Rheingold et al).

Focus on homicides tends to be on the victim who has lost their life, but little focus is given by society on those left behind. While this book focused on 32 murders, the close to 900 persons murdered over the past four decades have left dozens of family, friends and other loved ones who were impacted by their murder. The effects are worthy of discussion.

The murder of a family member leaves more than just bodies behind. Murder leaves survivors to struggle and cope with sudden and violent loss of life. The impact of violence on families, remains a complex issue. The degree to which children and adolescents are affected by it remains high. There are mental health consequences for those who are exposed to traumatic bereavement following a family member's homicide. Children tend to be overlooked in the grieving process. Research has shown that some psychological effects include anxiety, depression, post-traumatic stress disorder, aggression, guilt and a heightened sense of vulnerability. Socio-occupational effects include problems in school and at work. In Barbados, Minister of Education Santia Bradshaw revealed in August 2019 that recent research by the Ministry showed that children who lost loved ones to murder were acting out violently in schools across the island.

Besides the normal mourning process, co-victims having to cope with the loss of a loved one as a result of homicide also run the risk of developing Post Traumatic Stress Disorder (PTSD). A positive diagnosis of PTSD centres around the fact that the individual was exposed to a traumatic event in which he or she experienced, witnessed or was confronted with actual or threatened death or serious injury and the person's response involved intense fear, helplessness or horror (Burgess et al, 2010). Re-experiencing symptoms include intrusive thoughts, nightmares, feelings as if the event were recurring, and intense psychological and/or physiological distress at exposure to cues that trigger the event.

Avoidance symptoms include efforts to avoid thoughts or stimuli that are reminiscent of the event, avoiding people and places that cause distress, inability to recall important aspects of the event and feelings of detachment.

Arousal symptoms include difficulty falling asleep, emotional outbursts, difficulty concentrating, hypervigilance and exaggerated startled responses.

This may mean a more problematic mourning process than for those who have lost someone close due to a natural death (Parkes, 1993). Moreover, women experience more intensive grief symptoms than men (Sharpe et al., 2014). Co-victims also run a higher risk of long-term depression (Kaltman and Bonanno, 2003; Rheingold and Williams, 2015).

These feelings most likely occurred with those in this book who survived a violent attack or homicide, such as the lover of Mark Bryan, the roommate of Arlene Watts, the children and other neighbours who survived the Happy Cot and Haggatts tragedy; the survivors of the Campus Trendz fire, and their friends and other loved ones who came to the scene and tried valiantly to save their lives.

Other studies have shown that family members and friends of victims of homicide and other crimes often feel that they have little control over the criminal justice process or results. They felt left out of the investigation process, they are not updated on the status of the case, they are not given enough support as victims, there is no victim compensation fund for surviving family members and complain that they are generally forgotten by the criminal justice system.

In conclusion, homicide is a complex phenomenon usually driven by social situations. Mental illness, revenge, robberies and criminal opportunity that present themselves are all factors associated with homicides.

While we have seen a shift in the nature of homicides, and the predatory gruesome nature of these crimes, gun violence among young males is causing great concern in the region and in the world. Those who are at risk of antisocial behaviour must be targeted for effective social interventions.

Each murder leaves an immeasurable toll on those who have been left to mourn. The remaining victims, impacted by the crime, struggle to make sense of the sudden loss which has derailed their lives. However, too often, the focus is on the offender while the victim is forgotten in the process. We must do more work with victims to return their lives to some degree of normalcy, and more resources should be provided to them to assist in their rehabilitation efforts.

APPENDIX ONE

The Cane-Field Murders
Night of the Gathering Fields

Here The cane fields silently loom,
Dark and ominous under the moon,
Its roots, the remnants of scattered tombs,
Flesh and bones, an unfortunate doom.
Something's in the shadows, whisper ghostly cries,
He'll bring you here, where you will die,
Cold and alone, your corpse lay bare,
After he traps you within his snare.

Whispers from its depths, of unfortunate souls,
Stench of death rising, from its dismal hold,
Lonely spirits stare, behind the dancing blades,
Waiting for justice come judgment day.

The fields are quenched, filled for the night,
The wind and canes waltz with silent delight,
In the sky above , darkness slowly fades,
As dawns early light cast it's fresh shade.

So mothers and daughters you better beware,
Of the monster in the canes, in the fields of fear,
He'll swoons you, trick you, with a smile so dear,
The hour has cometh, your death is near.

Up to this day he has never been found,
Flew from these shores, was the talk around town,
Is he alive, or could he be dead,
Or continuing his serial path of dread.

The echoes still ripple of those frightful times,
As history bore witness, in memory it chimes,
To those who watched and baited his trail,
You were so close, but failure prevailed.

Was it your fault, no one will know,
A call was made to let him go.
To the survivor, you ran your tiring mile,
To the departed, rest easy my dear child.

Andrew Power